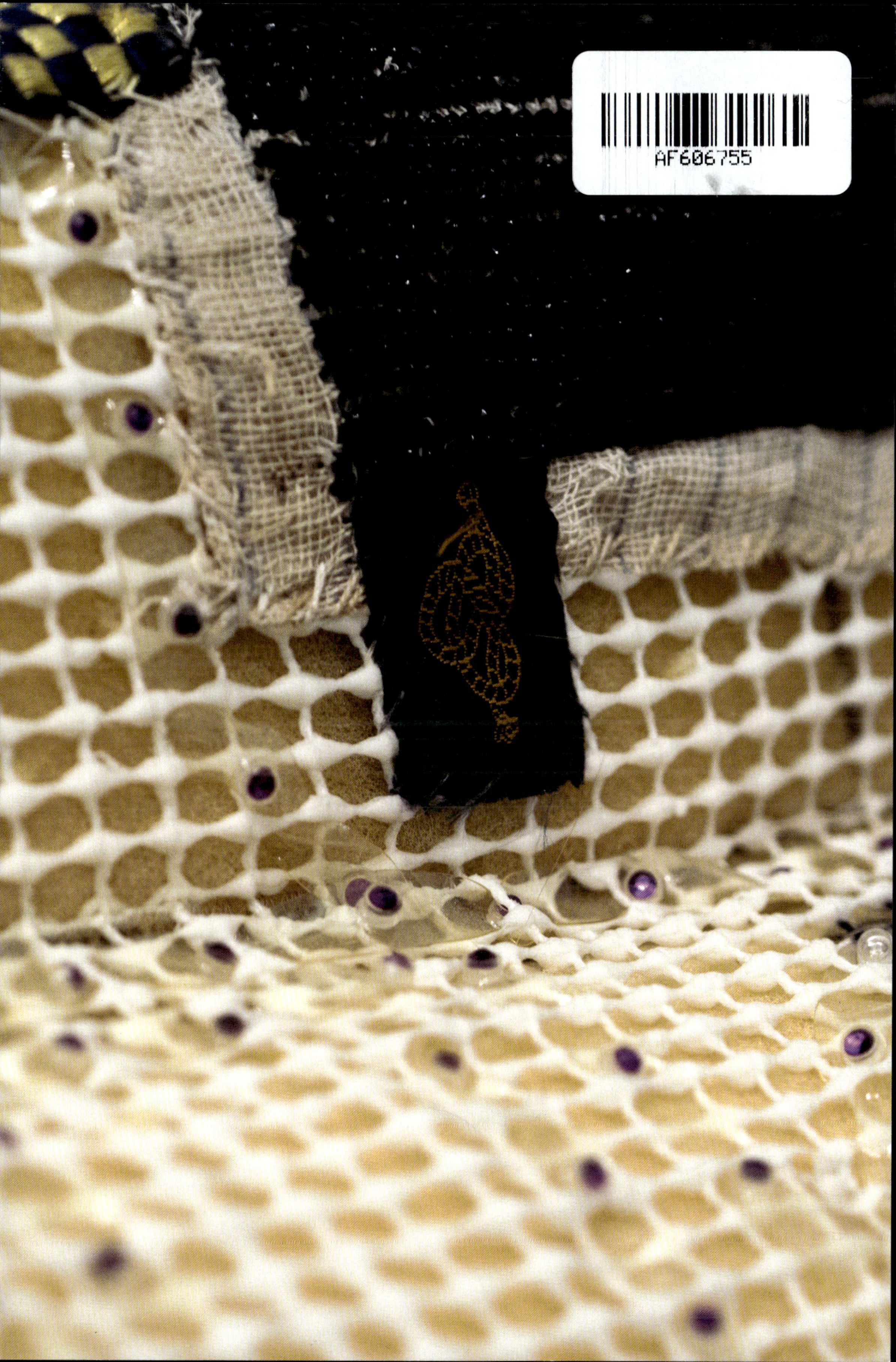

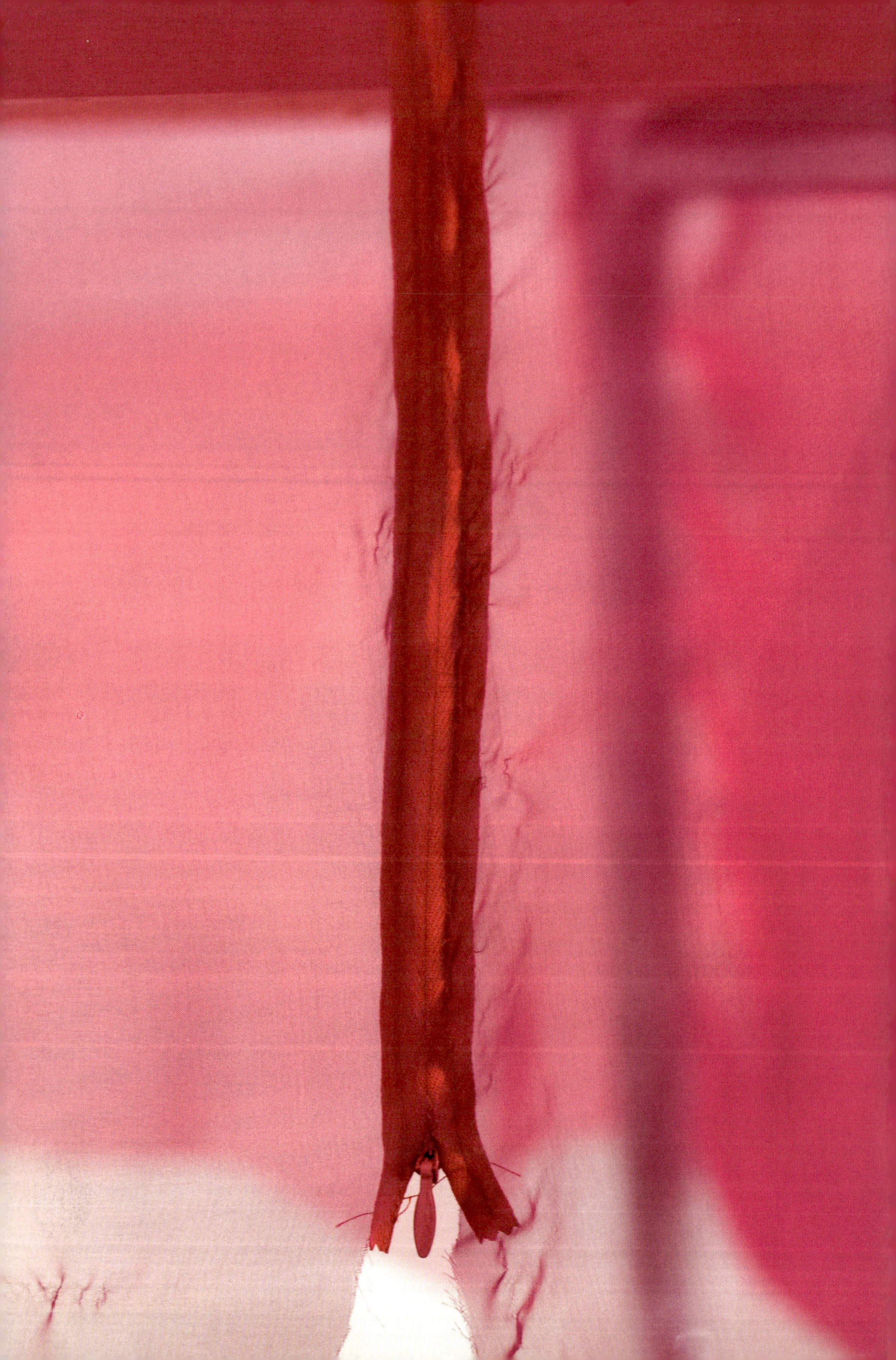

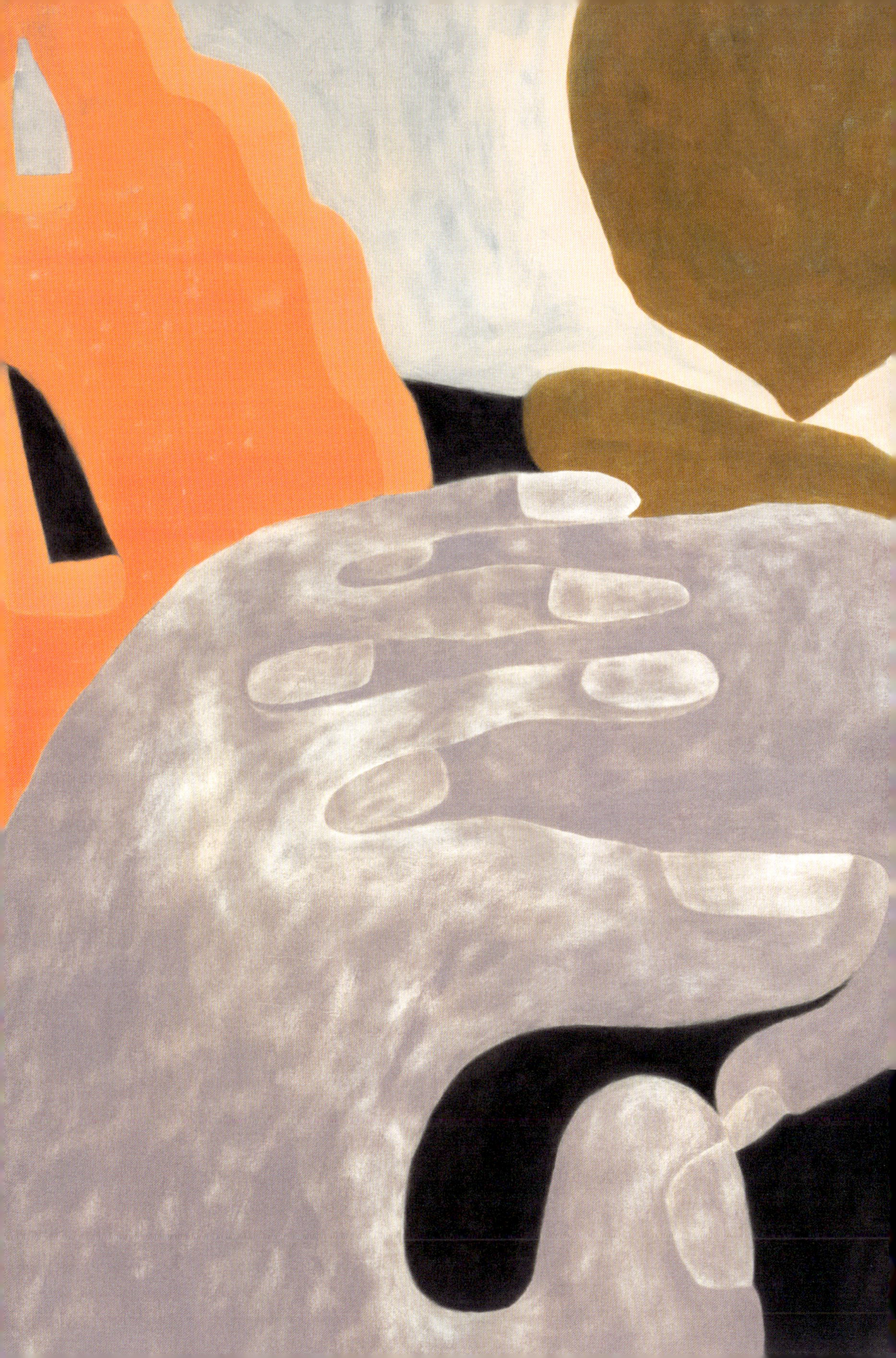

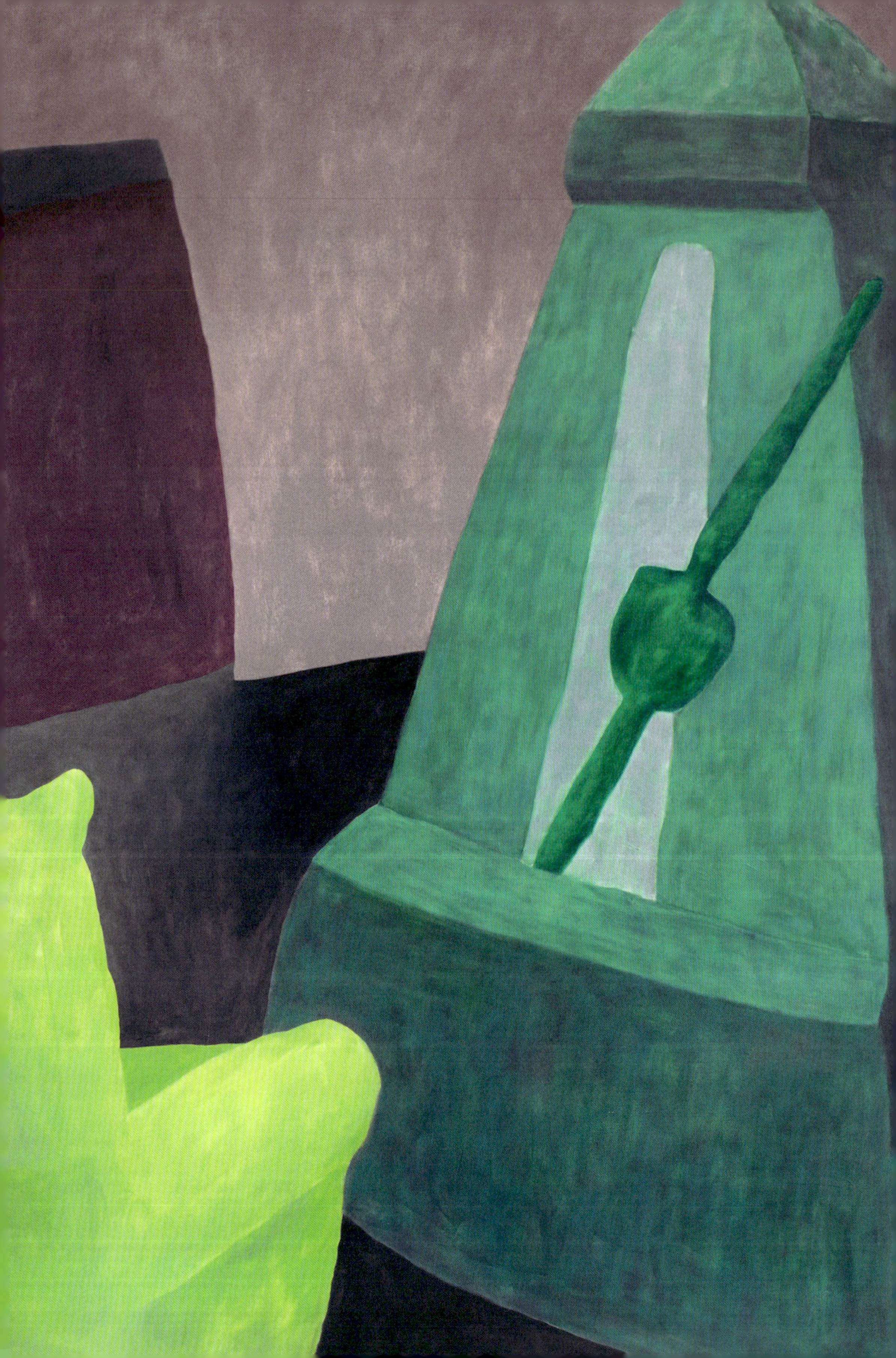

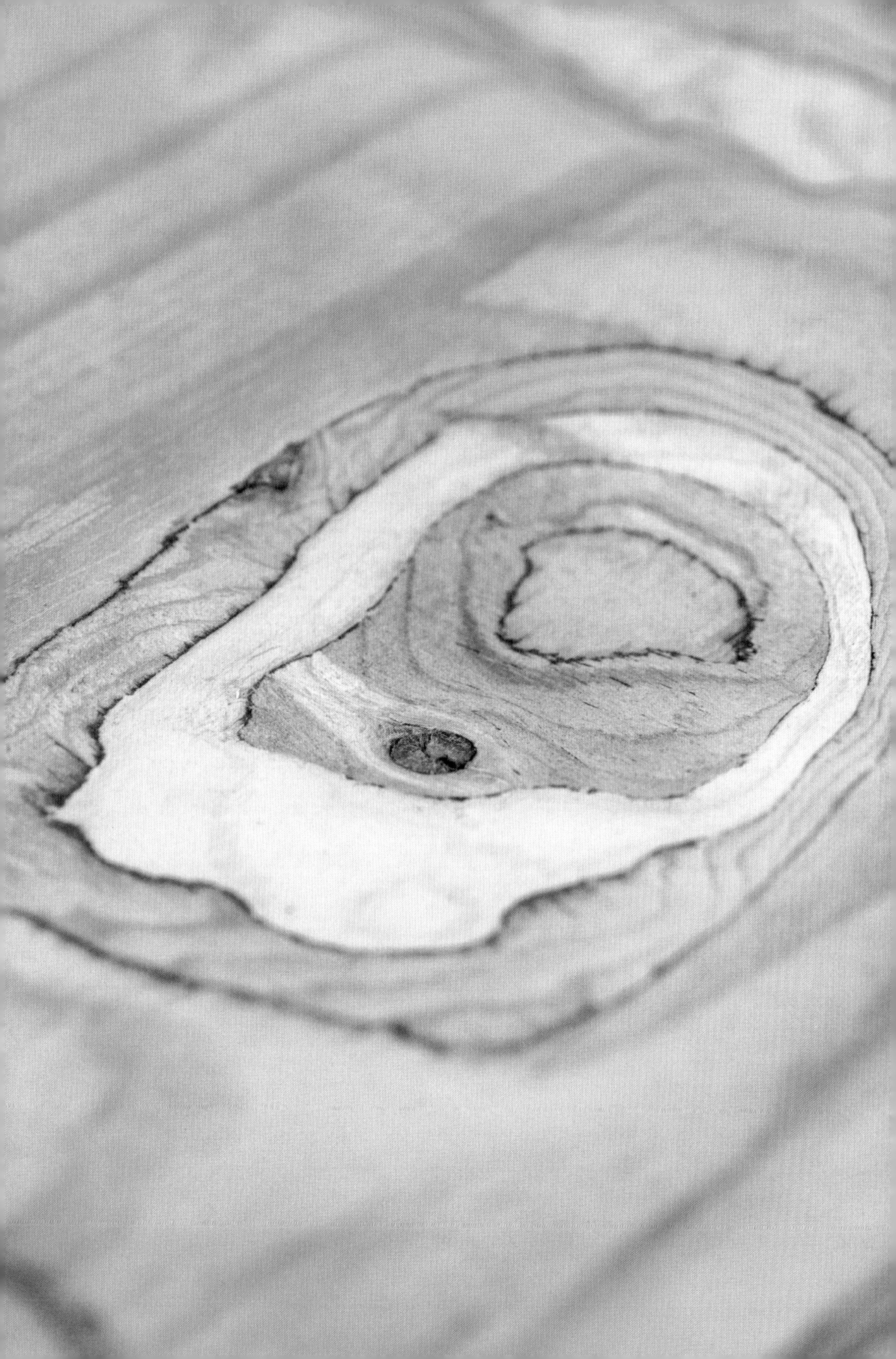

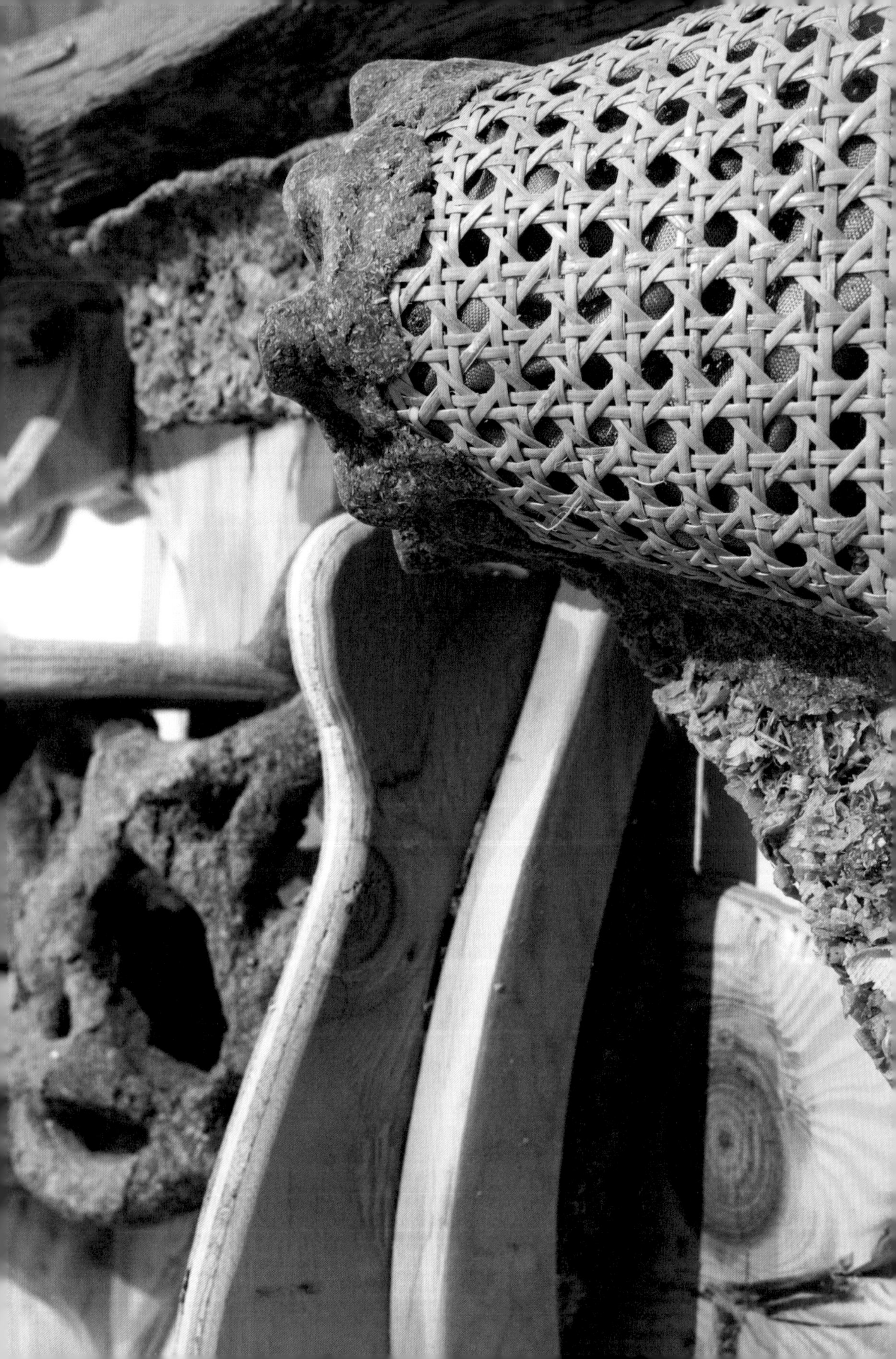

Ginny Casey

Jessi Reaves

Institute of Contemporary Art
University of Pennsylvania, Philadelphia

Contents

Director's Foreword

Amy Sadao

The pairing of Ginny Casey and Jessi Reaves exemplifies a whole that is greater, and significantly more unexpected, than its parts. Charlotte Ickes introduced the artists and deftly fomented the collaborative installation of their work. The resulting exhibition wittily sets our preconceptions about gallery viewing askew.

For their extraordinary work, I thank artists Jessi Reaves and Ginny Casey. Bridget Donahue, Erin Leland, and Thomas Barger were essential to our presentation of Jessi Reaves. Likewise, we thank Bill Powers, Erin Goldberger, and Jon Lutz for making Ginny Casey's participation possible. At ICA, I offer special recognition for the installation team of Paul Swenbeck, Mandy Bartram, Robert Chaney, and Patrick Maguire and the invaluable work of Greg Biche, Emelia Brintnall, Isabel Bump, Emily Elliot, Joy Feasley, Jake Kehs, Thom Lessner, Isaac Lin, Preston Link, Adam Lovitz, Jacob Lunderby, Samuel Margai, Julia Policastro, Sophie White, and Turner Williams.

James Goggin's book design with William Sumrall, Constance Mensh's photography, and Julia Bryan-Wilson's essay deserve special recognition. As do Other Means for creating innovative exhibition materials and ICA intern Joya Mandel-Assael who heroically enabled securing images rights.

Charlotte Ickes has been an extraordinary colleague over the past two years. For this publication and for creating important and challenging projects at ICA, I offer her my heartfelt thanks. Finally, I thank Leonard Lauder for enabling ICA to continue the important Whitney-Lauder Curatorial Fellowship pairing ICA with emerging curatorial talent.

The Surface of Stuff
The Stuff of Surface

Charlotte Ickes

And thus began the rule of the upholsterer,
a reign of terror that still gives us nightmares.
Adolf Loos,
"Interior Design: Prelude" (1898)[1]

Consequently if our work embodies
these beliefs, it must insult anyone
who is spiritually attuned to
interior decoration; pictures for the
home; pictures for over the mantle.
Letter to the *New York Times* by
Mark Rothko and Adolph Gottlieb (1943)[2]

When organizing a small exhibition at the
Whitney Museum of American Art some
years ago, it occurred to me that curatorial
display might be understood as a glorified
form of interior decoration.
Richard Meyer, "Big, Middle-Class
Modernism" (2010)[3]

As suggested in the title, Ginny Casey's painting *Sculpture Studio*, 2016, imagines the inside of a sculptor's workspace (fig. 1). I say "imagines" because Casey remains strictly a painter, and her actual studio couldn't be mistaken for anything but one of a painter, filled with easels and canvases as well as tables and brushes covered in chunks and dabs of oil paint. In this particular work, an array of semi-abstract, three-dimensional objects—perhaps of the ornamental sort you might find displayed on a bookshelf or coffee table—eagerly crowds the foreground, pressed up against the surface of the canvas. These objects appear almost animated, as do many of the everyday things populating her work. Even Casey's canvases quiver with life. Often sanded down or aggressively scrubbed with a drybrush, her

1 Adolf Loos, "Interior Design: Prelude," in *Ornament and Crime: Selected Essays*, trans. Michael Mitchell (Riverside, CA: Ariadne Press, 1998), 52.

2 Mark Rothko and Adolph Gottlieb, quoted in Bonnie Clearwater, "Shared Myths: Reconsideration of Rothko's and Gottlieb's Letter to the New York Times," *Archives of American Art Journal* 24 no. 1 (1984), 23.

3 Richard Meyer, "Big, Middle-Class Modernism," *October* 131 (Winter 2010), 69.

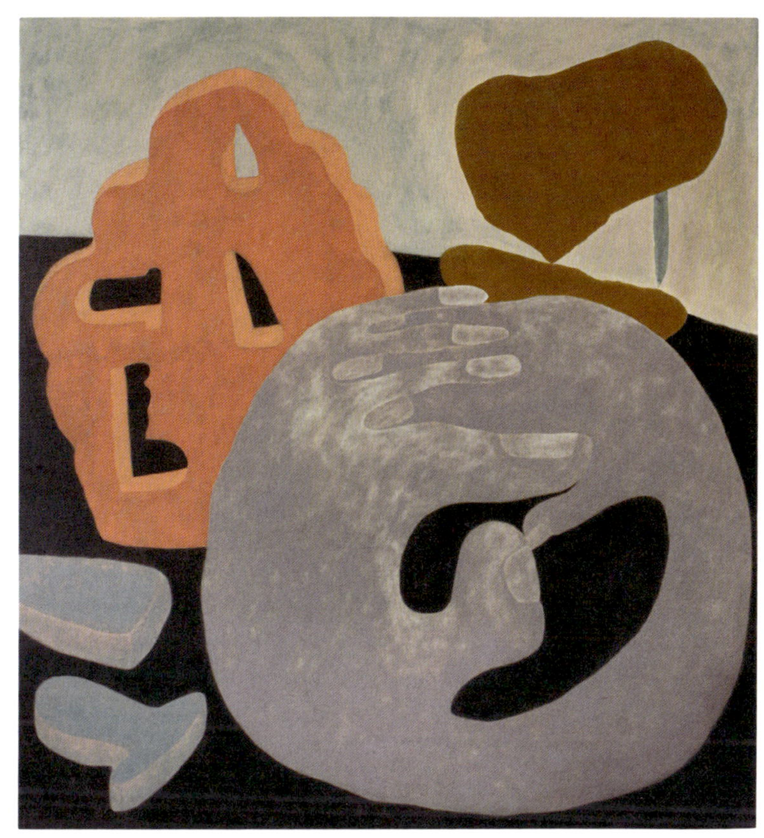

1
Ginny Casey, *Sculpture Studio*, 2016
Oil on canvas, 56 × 53 in.

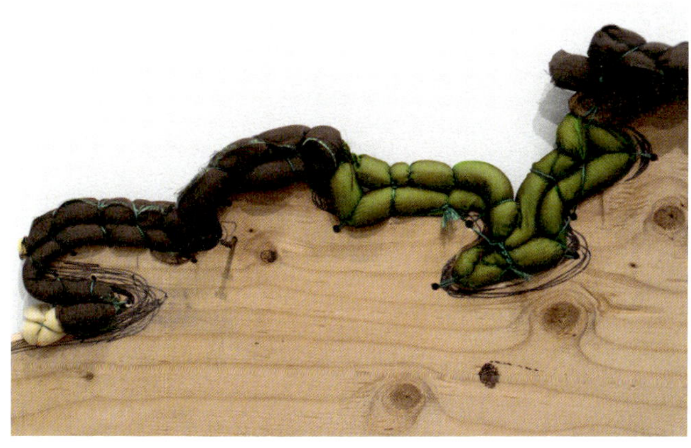

2
Jessi Reaves, *More Personal Headboard*, detail, 2017
Plywood, sawdust, wood glue, foam,
silk, nylon cord, ink, and wood putty,
24 × 98 × 13½ in.

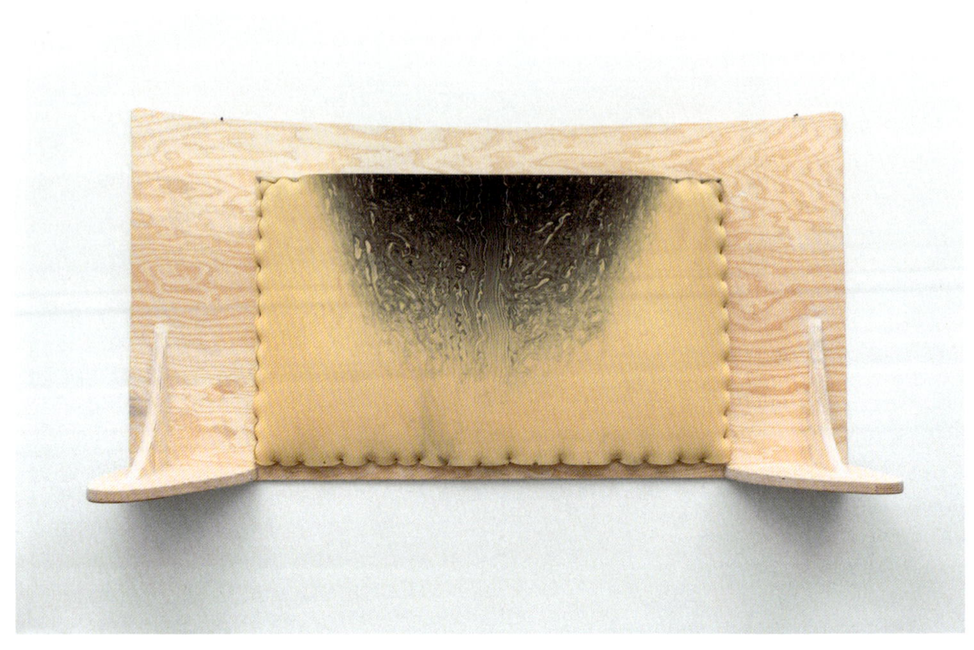

3
Jessi Reaves, *Anyone Knows How It Happened (Headboard for One)*, 2016
Plywood, foam and plastiwood, hardware, 48 × 94 × 19 in.

paintings acquire textures that might be ascribed to three-dimensional, rather than two-dimensional, objects. The artist "builds sculpture with paint," in her words, both in terms of what she depicts and how she depicts it.[4]

Although she once studied painting, Jessi Reaves makes sculptures that loudly proclaim their three-dimensional status. Customarily constructed from found frames of chairs, chaises, and shelves, Reaves's sculptures showcase her dexterity with a wide variety of textures, from sawdust to rattan to lumpy upholsterer's foam, a material familiar to the artist, who formerly worked part-time as an upholsterer. Although her works double as sculptures and functional furniture, their imperfect or embellished surfaces—the dark knots of wood peppering the flat plane of *More Personal Headboard*, 2017, stained foam of *Anyone Knows How It Happened (Headboard for One)*, 2016, chair cane recalling Picasso's Cubist pictures in *Shelf for a Log*, 2016, and patterned fabric of *Chair 1*, 2016, and *Chair 2*, 2016—also accommodate pictorial aspirations and ornamental excess that surpass these objects' original use (figs. 2, 3, 4, 5).

Casey's paintings and Reaves's sculptures meet on and through the language of decorative and domestic objects, found in the home but here endowed with lives of their own.[5] This encounter runs contrary to how art and design have often been understood in relation to domestic decoration, which is to say, on opposing terms.[6] Architect Adolf Loos's disdain for the "rule of the upholsterer" and overstuffed furniture popular during the Victorian era exemplifies this rift, as does abstract artists Mark Rothko's and Adolph Gottlieb's contempt for the mere suggestion that their canvases could resemble "interior decoration" almost half a century later. As Loos, Rothko, and Gottlieb explicitly tell us, decoration in many ways maintained a subordinate position within the orbit of modernism in art, architecture, and design. And it still does to a certain extent, with the publication of Hal Foster's *Design and Crime*, 2002, for example, named after Loos's notorious manifesto "Ornament and

4 Ginny Casey, conversation with the author, September 23, 2016.

5 De Stijl, founded in 1917 by Theo van Doesburg, is an important historical touchstone for the marriage of architecture, design, painting, and sculpture. De Stijl was invested in a total abstract interior through the language of "pure color" as a "proposal for the future" and "means of social change," in Nancy Troy's words. There are many differences between De Stijl's thought and practice and *Ginny Casey & Jessi Reaves*, in particular De Stijl's "severe stylistic purity," commitment to abstraction, and De Stijl's painters' disdain for decoration, but it serves as a significant example of how painting, sculpture, and interior space have intersected. For more information, see Nancy Troy, *The De Stijl Environment* (Cambridge, MA: The MIT Press, 1983), 2-3, 5, 138.

6 Ibid., 69-71; Helen Molesworth, "Louise Lawler: Just the Facts," in *Interiors: CCS Readers: Perspectives on Art and Culture*, eds. Johanna Burton, Lynne Cooke, and Josiah McElheny (Annandale-on-Hudson, NY: Center for Curatorial Studies, Bard College/Sternberg Press, 2012).

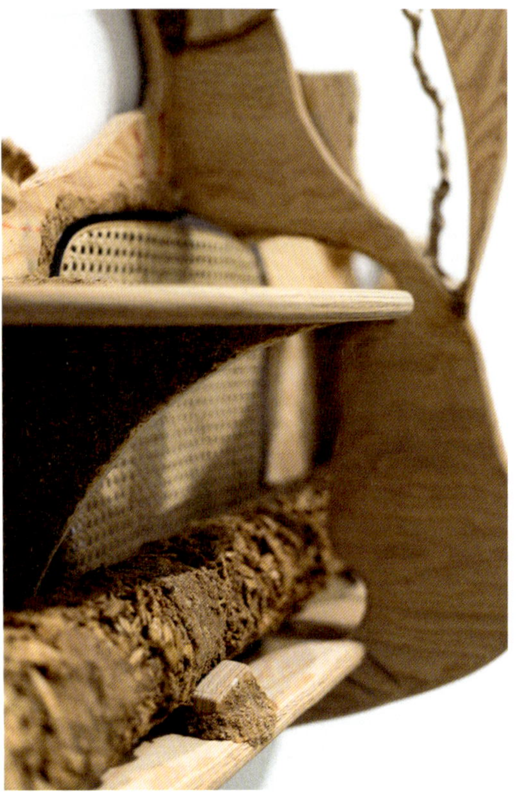

4
Jessi Reaves, *Shelf for a Log*, detail, 2016
Plywood, sawdust, cane chair
seat, and ink, 34 × 68 × 13 in.

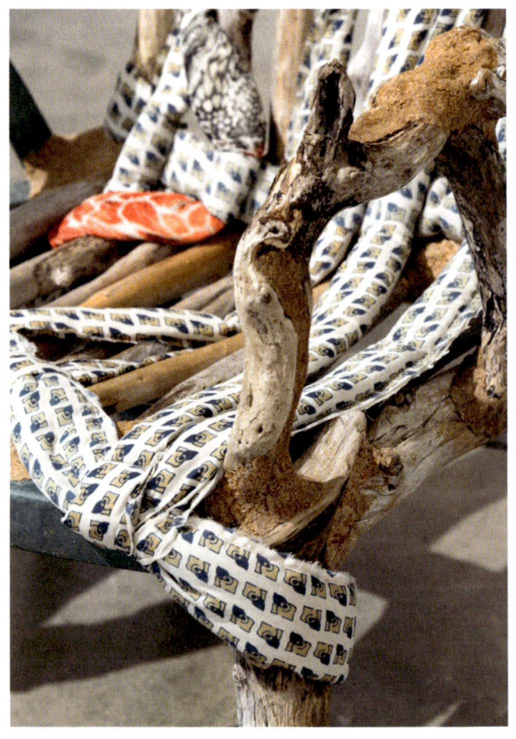

5
Jessi Reaves, *Chair 1*, detail, 2016
Plastic, driftwood, sawdust, wood glue,
fabric, cotton batting, and polyurethane foam,
38 × 25 × 29 in.

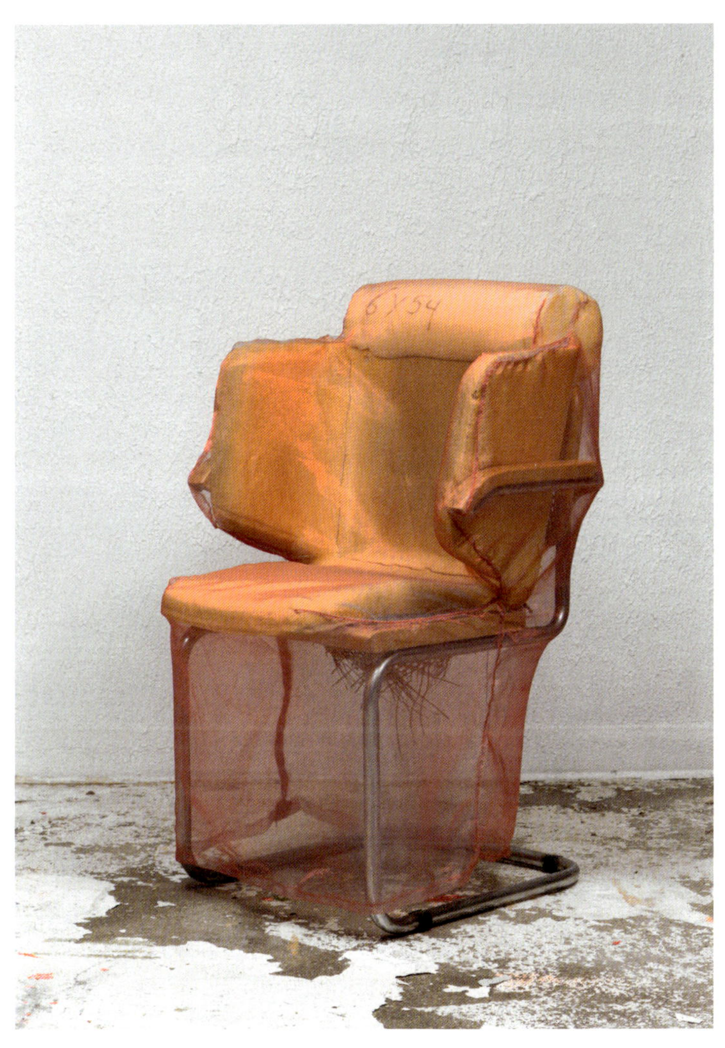

6

Jessi Reaves, *Cesca Leaves the Stack (Modified Chair)*, 2016
Polyurethane foam, tubular steel frame chrome plated finish, hardwood beech with cane inserts, rayon, nylon, plastic, ink, and hardware, 48 × 18½ × 28 in.

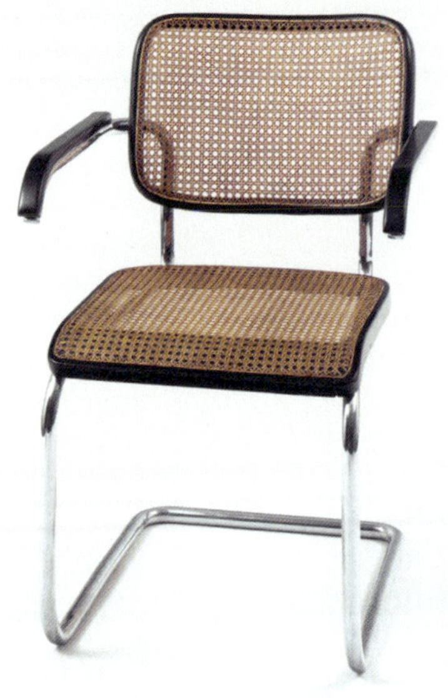

7
Marcel Breuer, Cesca Armchair (model B64), 1928
Bent chromed tubular steel, wood, and cane,
30⅞ × 22⅞ × 23¼ in.

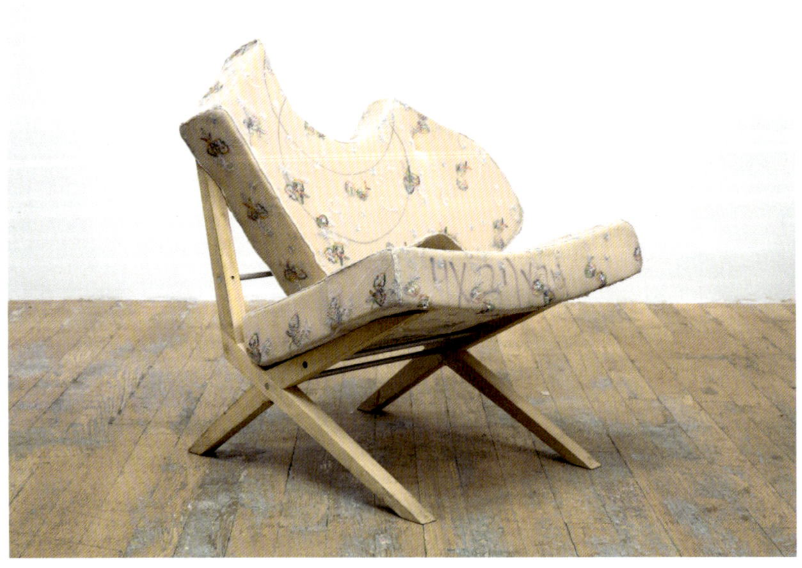

8
Jessi Reaves, *if you want to know what will bring you back to life, it's nothing*, 2014
Wood, foam, nylon, beads, piping, and pearls,
39 × 94 × 19 in.

Crime", 1908, which, in Foster's words, "attacked the indiscriminate spread of ornament in all things."[7] Moreover, much modernist discourse on decoration pivoted around gender. Certain registers of symbolic femininity, such as sensuality and superficiality, became negatively equated with the excessive, embellished surfaces of upholstered furniture and ornamental objects in the home, the historical locus of women's work.[8]

What if, however, we were to take seriously domestic space and all the things, large and small, arranged in it? "What if "pictures for the home" were not so wildly different from pictures for the gallery, and the "rule of the upholsterer" was one likewise followed by the sculptor? What if Richard Meyer is right, and interior decorating and exhibition installation have more similarities than differences, particularly when an exhibition includes sculptures that function as furniture from which to view paintings that depict chairs, tables, vases, fans, and all manner of other humble objects? And what if these objects remained humble in their quotidian function and at the same time acquired an unexpected enchantment?

"Decoration can be said to be the specter that haunts modernist painting," or a Slipcovered Chair and a Droopy Vase[9]

Modern furniture design quite literally serves as the armature of Reaves's work. Take *Cesca Leaves the Stack (Modified Chair)*, 2016, which reworks Marcel Breuer's B64, 1928 (figs. 6, 7). The artist "modifies" this modernist icon with semitransparent nylon, a decorative surface through which to glimpse the structure underneath. The fabric tints the chair with a rosy hue, adding an element of romance to

7 Hal Foster, *Design and Crime* (London; New York: Verso, 2002), xiv; Adolf Loos, "Ornament and Crime," in *Ornament and Crime: Selected Essays*, trans. Michael Mitchell (Riverside, CA: Ariadne Press, 1998). Ironically, the interior of Loos's own home, in particular his wife's bedroom, was covered in plush fabrics. For more information, see Beatriz Colomina, "The Split Wall: Domestic Voyeurism," in *Sexuality & Space*, ed. Beatriz Colomina (New York: Princeton Architectural Press, 1992), 92; Anne Cheng, "Skin, Tattoos, and Susceptibility," *Representations* 108, no. 1 (Fall 2009), 104.

8 Meyer, "Big, Middle-Class Modernism," 70; Penny Sparke, "Introduction," in *Interior Design and Identity*, eds. Susie McKellar and Penny Sparke (Manchester: Manchester University Press, 2004), 3-7; Penny Sparke, *The Modern Interior* (London: Reaktion, 2008), 13-15; Naomi Schor, *Reading in Detail: Aesthetics and the Feminine* (New York: Methuen, 1987), 47-53.

9 Clement Greenberg, "Milton Avery," in *Art and Culture: Critical Essays* (Boston: Beacon Press, 1989), 200.

Breuer's tubular-steel-and-cane construction while poking some fun at the high seriousness of his structure. The found foam over the seat further obscures our view of the chair's geometry and increases the range of textures available in this work. Reaves's additions are structurally unnecessary as ornamental supplements that provide little to no functional improvement. But they do alter the chair's formal and symbolic vocabularies. The artist covers the chair with a distinctly feminine scrim as a woman might cover her legs with nylons, and chooses to acknowledge the real woman behind the alternative title, "Cesca," named after Breuer's daughter, Francesca.[10]

The artist has frequently covered her sculptures with transparent fabric, resulting in the unexpected eroticism of a supposedly inanimate, everyday object. In *if you want to know what will bring you back to life, it's nothing*, 2014, Reaves layers found foam cushions, scuffed with an upholsterer's cut marks, on top of a generic modernist frame (fig. 8). She wraps the cushions with transparent fabric embroidered with beading, an effect the artist likens to "seeing someone's pubic hair through sexy lingerie."[11] Reaves's evocative description anthropomorphizes her sculptural furniture and surface interventions with reference to both the female body *and* a woman's "sexy" bedroom garments. For the exhibition at the ICA, Reaves dressed another B64 with semi-transparent magenta fabric. The title of this new work, *Slipcovered Chair (Pink Gag)*, 2017, alludes to the "gag" played at Breuer's expense: the raggedy edges of the pink fabric contrast with the sleek lines of the chair's construction while the zipper and sweetly decorative trim dress the chair with a gratuitous "slipcover" (fig. 9).

Two years after Breuer debuted his first tubular-steel armchair, he noted that the design's positive reception "showed me clearly that contemporary attitudes were undergoing a change, abandoning the whimsical in favour

10 Otakar Marcel, "Marcel Breuer—'Inventor of Bent Tubular Steel Furniture,'" in *Marcel Breuer: Design and Architecture* (Weil am Rhein: Vitra Design Museum, 2003), 92; The Museum of Modern Art website, "Marcel Breuer, Cesca Armchair (model B64), 1928," accessed May 18, 2017, www.moma.org/collection/works/2814.

11 Jessi Reaves, quoted in Julia Trotta, "Scrap Queen," *PIN-UP* no. 19 (Fall/Winter 2015/16), 52-53.

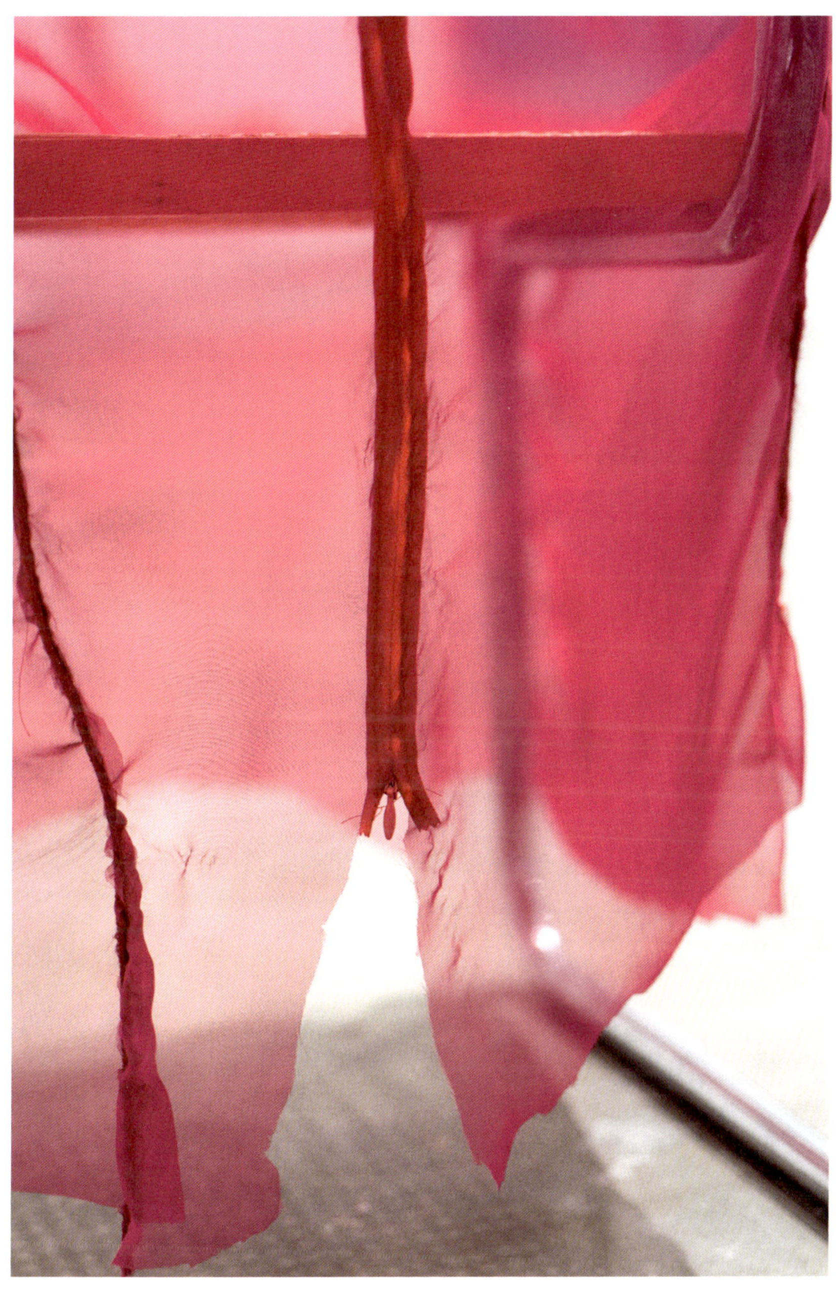

9
Jessi Reaves, *Slipcovered Chair (Pink Gag)*, detail, 2017
Found chair, fabric, zipper, and thread, 33 × 22 × 24 in.

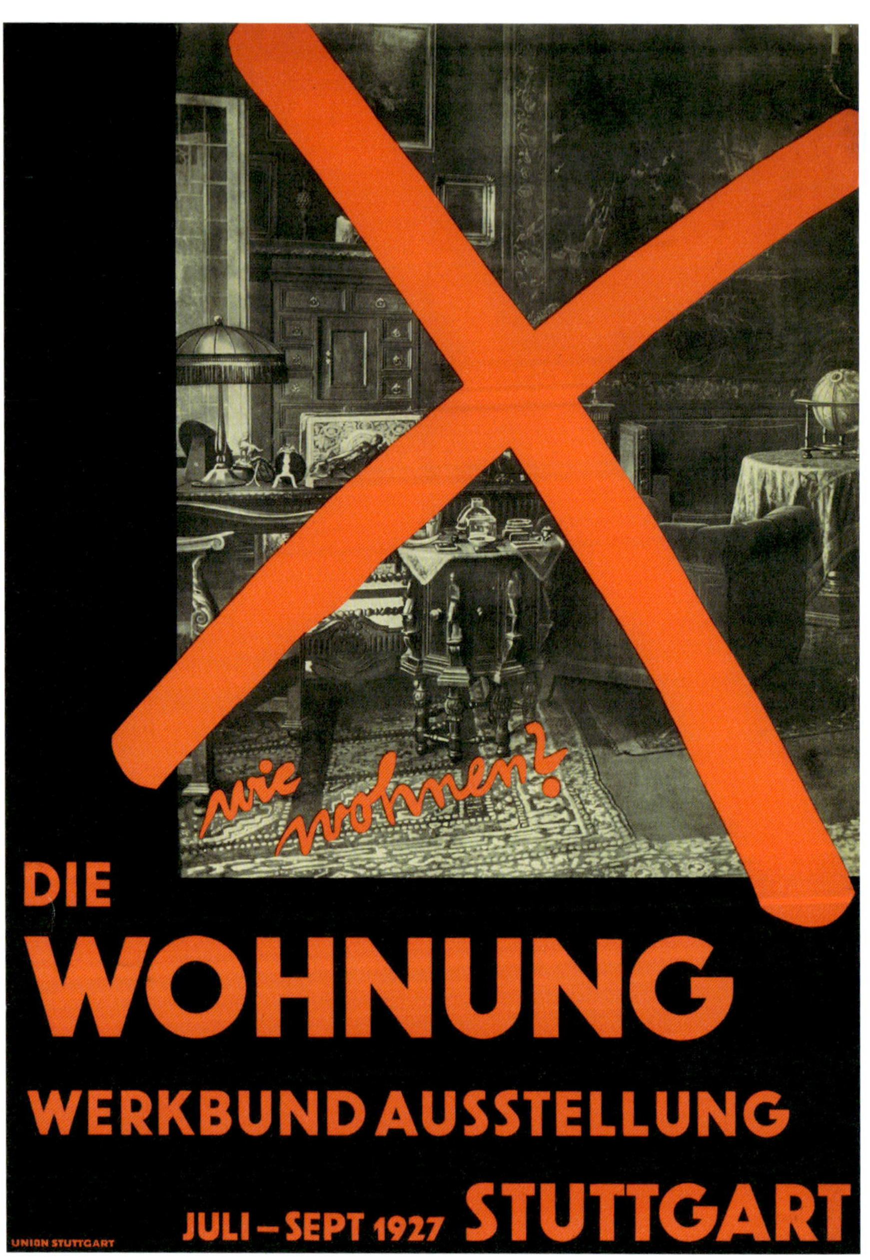

10
Willi Baumeister, *Wie wohnen? Die Wohnung: Werkbund Ausstellung*, 1927
Offset lithograph, 44¾ × 32⅜ × 23¼

of the rational."[12] Breuer's emphasis on rational thought and unadorned structures derives from his experience as a student and teacher at the Bauhaus, the German school founded in 1919 to unite the arts into an integrated curriculum.[13] Much industrial design emerged from the Bauhaus, in many ways geared toward the standardized promise of the machine, rational scientific thought, functionalism as well as mass-market appeal and affordability.[14] What resulted were unembellished structures that prioritized efficiency, function, and relatively inexpensive materials such as tubular steel, first used in Breuer's 1925 club armchair and later in the B64.[15] In addition to the Bauhaus, the Deutscher Werkbund, an association of artists, craftsmen, designers, architects, and manufacturers founded in 1907, helped spread the ethos of functionalism in the first part of the twentieth century. A poster for *Die Wohnung* (The Dwelling), the 1927 Deutscher Werkbund exhibition in Stuttgart, shows in no uncertain terms exactly what these modernists desired to leave behind: a Victorian-era decorative schema overrun with ornamental objects, heavily upholstered furniture, and a riot of fabric, from tablecloths to rugs (fig. 10).[16] The abrupt crosshairs of an X slash this bourgeois domestic ideal, communicating a radical break from what Walter Benjamin considered to be a nineteenth-century obsession with interiors, interiority, and individualism in his native Europe. A "private environment" for a "private individual" was enclosed in "dense fabric" and "folds of velvet," a "womb," in Benjamin's gendered language, divorced from workplace and public space, generally reserved for men.[17] These mostly male *designers* aligned themselves with the worlds of industry and science, seeking to purge the bourgeois home of excessive

12 Marcel Breuer, quoted in George Marcus, *Functionalist Design: An Ongoing History* (New York; Munich: Prestel, 1995), 89.

13 Markus Bruderlin, "Introduction: Interior Exterior: The Modern Soul and the Search for the Ideal Home," in *Interieur, Exterieur—Living in Art: From Romantic Interior Painting to the Home Design of the Future* (Osfildern: Hatje Cantz, 2008), 207; Judith Miller, *Furniture: World Styles from Classical to Contemporary* (London: DK, 2005), 426.

14 Marcus, *Functionalist Design*, 57; Judith Gura, *Design After Modernism: Furniture and Interiors, 1970-2010* (New York: W. W. Norton, 2012), 11, 19.

15 Florence de Dampierre, *Chairs: A History* (New York: Abrams, 2006), 380; Mathias Remmele, "Marcel Breuer Design and Architecture—An Introduction," in *Marcel Breuer: Design and Architecture* (Weil am Rhein: Vitra Design Museum, 2003), 16-19.

16 Marcus, *Functionalist Design*, 67.

17 Walter Benjamin, "Paris, Capital of the Nineteenth Century," in *Walter Benjamin: Selected Writings Vol. 3, 1935-1938*, eds. Michael W. Jennings, Howard Eiland, and Gary Smith (Cambridge, MA; London: The Belknap Press of Harvard University Press, 1999), 38; Walter Benjamin, quoted in Diana Fuss, *The Sense of an Interior: Four Writers and the Rooms that Shaped Them* (New York: Routledge, 2004), 9.

ornament and surface treatments, the remnants of women who indulged what was dismissed as mere consumption habits of amateur *decorators*.[18]

Ludwig Mies van der Rohe, the third and final director of the Bauhaus, organized *Die Wohnung*, which also included the work of Breuer as well as Swiss architect, designer, and painter Le Corbusier.[19] Le Corbusier shared an interest in the machine and mass production, structure over surface, and universal forms. He wrote prolifically about eliminating unnecessary decoration from all aspects of modern living: "Why the enormous glass chandeliers? The mantelpieces? Why the draped curtains? Why the damasked wall-papers thick with colour with their motley design?"[20] Excessive decoration in the home reflected an overall lack of civilization, a racialized and classed reading of time, history, and progress espoused by Loos as well.[21] "Culture is the flowering of the effort to select," writes Le Corbusier in *Towards a New Architecture*, aping social Darwinism. "Selection means rejection, pruning, cleansing; the clear and naked emergence of the Essential."[22] Bare whitewashed walls and Platonic geometries constituted the "Essential" while the "accidental surface modality" of decoration reveled in the "superfluous."[23] Le Corbusier's critique of decoration as "something which only touches the surface" pivots, as Mark Wigley has shown, on his suspicion and fear not only of barbarism and the retardation of civilization but also of the feminine, materialized as a sensuous surface that threatens to overwhelm the rational faculties of man, the body exercising power over the mind.[24]

Compare Reaves's *Kragel's Nap Chair*, 2015, to the LC4, 1928, designed by Le Corbusier, Pierre Jeanneret, and Charlotte Perriand, who were inspired by lounges used by patients recovering from tuberculosis in sanatoriums

18 Sparke, *The Modern Interior*, 14-16, 21, 109, 188; Peter McNeil, "Designing Women: Gender, Sexuality, and the Interior Decoration, c. 1890-1940," *Art History* 17, no. 4 (December 1994), 637-39, 642; Nancy J. Troy, "Domesticity, Decoration and Consumer Culture: Selling Art and Design in Pre-WWI France," in *Not at Home: The Suppression of Domesticity in Modern Art and Architecture*, ed. Christopher Reed (London: Thames and Hudson, 1996), 116-17, 121-22.

19 Marcel, "Marcel Breuer—'Inventor of Bent Tubular Steel Furniture,'" 72.

20 Le Corbusier, *Towards a New Architecture*, trans. Frederick Etchells (New York: Dover Publications, Inc., 1986), 115.

21 Mark Wigley, *White Walls, Designer Dresses: The Fashioning of Modern Architecture* (Cambridge, MA: The MIT Press, 1995), 9; Troy, *The De Stijl Environment*, 178; Schor, *Reading in Detail*, 51.

22 Le Corbusier, *Towards a New Architecture*, 138.

23 Le Corbusier, *The Decorative Art of Today*, trans. James Dunnett (Cambridge, MA: The MIT Press, 1987), xxiv, 186.

24 Ibid., 114; Wigley, *White Walls, Designer Dresses*, 37, 191, 361.

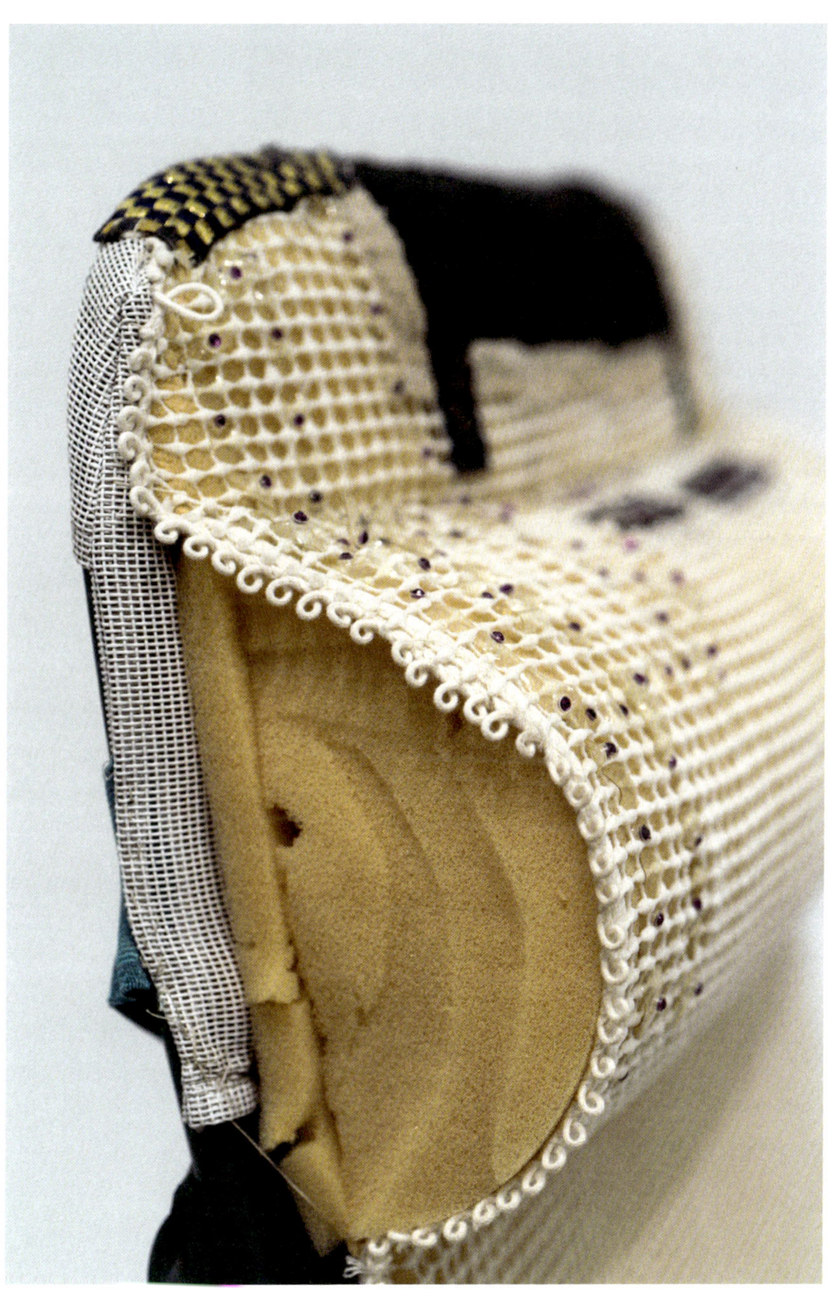

11
Jessi Reaves, *Kragel's Nap Chair*, detail, 2015
Steel, rattan, enamel, polyurethane foam, cotton, ink, plastic glass, and hardware, 47 × 24½ × 48 in.

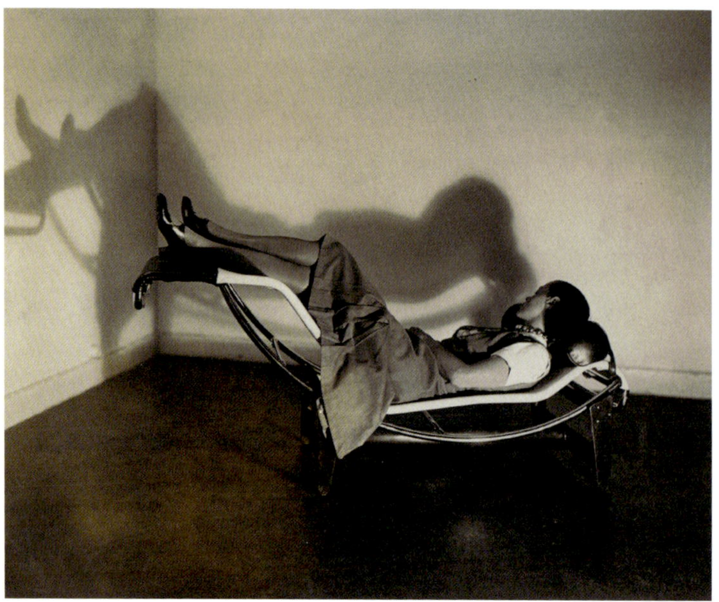

12
Charlotte Perriand, *Charlotte Perriand resting on the chaise longue*, 1928
Photograph. Designed by Le Corbusier, Charlotte Perriand, and Pierre Jeanneret

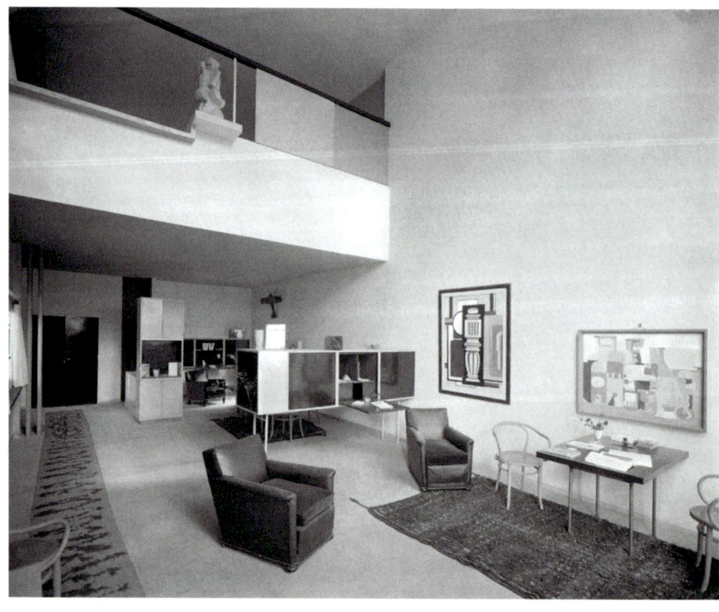

13
Pierre Jeanneret and Le Corbusier, Pavillion de l'Esprit Nouveau, 1925, *Exposition Internationale des Arts Décoratifs et Industriels Modernes*, Paris

(figs. 11, 12).[25] The soiled upholsterer's foam, frayed and fractured rattan, as well as ornamental beading and decorative decals, all exude contradictory registers of warmth, roughness, tenderness, and even an irresistible grotesque that diverge from the indifferent affect of the LC4's sleek chrome and leather. Integrating materials worn from everyday use, Reaves's work demands recognition of the object's own sensuous specificity and patina of making and unmaking, using and overusing, often unavailable in the universal geometries and seemingly ageless forms of modern design. Even the title serves as a rejoinder to Le Corbusier's unchanging and impersonal notion of the "Essential." "Kragel" is the artist's nickname for older people who might snooze in this lounge chair, itself a family relic as "kragely" as its imagined user.[26] If a "chair has no soul," as Le Corbusier declared, then Reaves's furniture might intimate otherwise.[27]

Universal geometries shaped Le Corbusier's approach to painting in addition to design. In 1918, he co-authored a theory of Purism as an alternative to what he deemed painting's decorative tendencies. As still-life compositions, Purist canvases depict simple machine-made objects or *objet types*, often bottles or other vessels that signified timeless design.[28] Stripped of detail as representative types, the ensemble of objects in Purist paintings demonstrates Le Corbusier's preference for mass-produced furniture with simple structures and unembellished surfaces, and an example of the confluence of Purist painting and modern furniture design can be seen in Le Corbusier's and Pierre Jeanneret's 1925 Pavillon de L'Esprit Nouveau, a model villa for the *Exposition International des Arts Décoratifs et Industriels Modernes* in Paris (fig 13).[29] Casey's canvases are also allied with the still-life tradition and elaborate upon basic geometries of circles, squares, and rectangles. Yet the objects in her scenes are far from timeless or robbed of particularly, and some look downright handcrafted. Casey paints unfolding actions and/or end results

25 Miller, *Furniture*, 420.

26 Jessi Reaves, conversation with the author, March 31, 2017.

27 Le Corbusier, *Towards a New Architecture*, 142.

28 Wigley, *White Walls, Designer Dresses*, 197; Troy, *The De Stijl Environment*, 178.

29 Charles Rice, *The Emergence of the Interior: Architecture, Modernity, Domesticity* (London; New York: Routledge, 2007), 105-106; Arthur Rüegg, *Le Corbusier: Furniture and Interiors, 1905-1965* (Paris: Foundation Le Corbusier, 2012), 9, 250; George H. Marcus, *Le Corbusier: Inside the Machine for Living: Furniture and Interiors* (New York: Monacelli Press, 2000), 45.

of prior events that often involve destruction, just as the odd combination of materials in Reaves's work records her own effort of construction, reconstruction, and deconstruction. A saw is caught slicing a table in Casey's *Blue Table*, 2016, for instance. A whiff of narrative emerges from the fractured remains of a vase lying on a table near a hammer in the painting *Broken Vase*, 2015. And time itself is represented by an oversize metronome in *Keeping Time*, 2017 (fig. 14). Moreover, from the ornamental skirts on each end of the table in *Blue Table* to the muscular curls of a vase's lip in *Droopy Vase*, 2015, Casey has allotted decorative attributes to these objects, distinguishing them from the anonymity of industrial production (fig. 15). Their unique status is underscored by the fact that the artist has included references to handicraft, such as pottery or sculpting tools.

The lived-in textures of Reaves's sculptures and the spirited objects in Casey's paintings lay bare the difference between their work and modernist art and design. At the same time, they also perhaps elicit what modernism has suppressed: the ornamental decoration and sensual surfaces upon whose erasure modernism structurally depends. The tension between structure and surface within modern architecture and design is made plain in the image of Charlotte Perriand luxuriating on the LC4 she helped create. She is pictured here as both model *and* designer. The sleek gleam of chrome and leather are still on full display, but so are the dramatic shadows and Baroque fold of her skirt draped across the chaise, shoring up an earlier version of the piece that employed ponyskin.[30] "The problem is not the feminine per se, but the feminine within the masculine," writes Wigley on Le Corbusier. "The public image of masculine control is produced by the private mastery of the stereotypically feminine art of the surface," he continues.[31] As Wigley points out, Le Corbusier's prolific use of white paint is itself a decorative choice rather than a neutral

30 Marcus, *Functionalist Design*, 104; Rüegg, *Le Corbusier*, 283-84.

31 Wigley, *White Walls, Designer Dresses*, 361,32

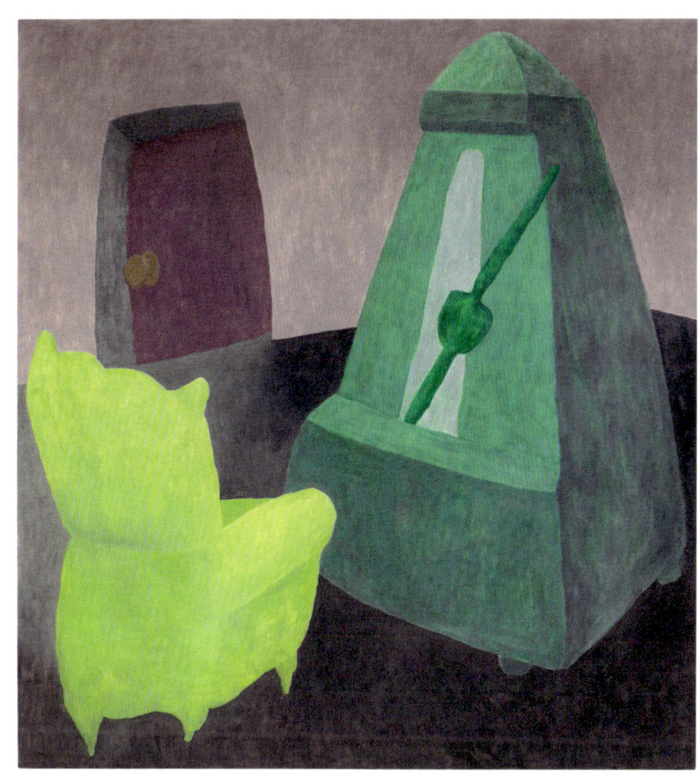

14
Ginny Casey, *Keeping Time*, 2017
Oil on canvas, 70 × 65 in.

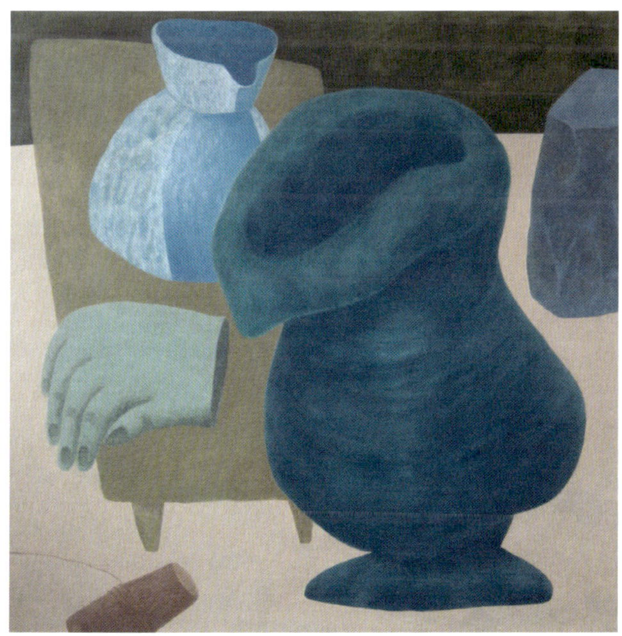

15
Ginny Casey, *Droopy Vase*, 2015
Oil on canvas, 55 × 55 in.

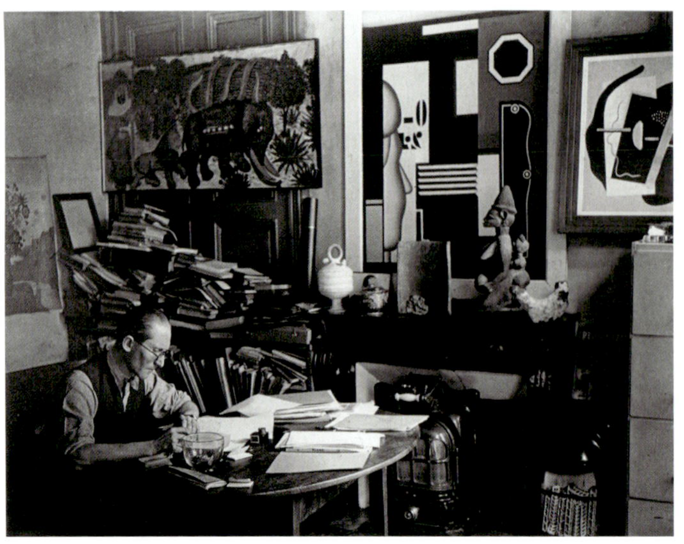

16
Brassaï, *Le Corbusier at his work table, rue Jacob*, 1931
Photograph.

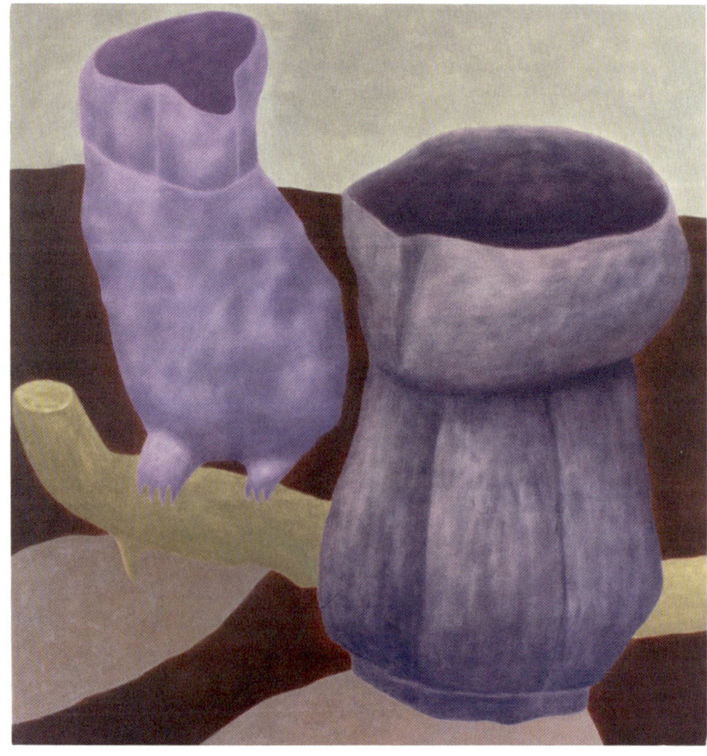

17
Ginny Casey, *Purple Conversation*, 2016
Oil on canvas, 32 × 30 in.

given, and he urges us to remember that Le Corbusier initially trained in the decorative arts and previously worked as an interior decorator.[32] Even in his own home, Le Corbusier fails to heed his advice to "demand bare walls" and "never buy decorative pieces."[33] Brassaï's 1930 photograph of the architect's apartment shows him surrounded by piles of books and papers (fig. 16). Paintings cover almost every available surface, and Le Corbusier's "*collection particulière*," or "collection of bric-a-brac," in Brassaï's less forgiving terms, crowds the fireplace mantle.[34] What critic Clement Greenberg, champion of midcentury Abstract Expressionists such as Rothko and Gottlieb, once said about the relationship between decoration and modern painting could equally apply to this photograph of Le Corbusier's endearingly cluttered apartment. "Decoration," wrote Greenberg, "can be said to be the specter that haunts modernist painting."[35] Casey's and Reaves's practices take an unlikely itinerary through overlooked and alternative art and design histories, critically reminding us that the sensual surfaces and ornamental objects of interior decoration inhabit and even haunt modernism: the Charlotte in the LC4, the Cesca in the B64, the paintings over the mantle, the "bric-a-brac" decorating it.

"The chair will have life," or a Butt Table and Chatty Forms[36]

Casey's *Purple Conversation*, 2016, shows two vessels resembling owls engaged in dialogue (fig. 17). The smaller vase, painted in an Easter-egg purple, perches on a branch, cocking its head toward its larger conversation partner positioned in the foreground. Reaves's *Dog's Toy Coat Rack*, 2015, similarly invokes animal life (fig. 18). According to the artist, the piece earned its title from the chipped and gnarled surface of the oak, which appears as if a

32 Ibid., xiv–xvi, xviii, 180.

33 Le Corbusier, *Towards a New Architecture*, 123.

34 Le Corbusier and Brassaï, quoted in Rüegg, *Le Corbusier*, 127.

35 Greenberg, "Milton Avery," 200.

36 Salvador Dalí, quoted in Ghislaine Wood, "The Illusory Interior," in *Surreal Things: Surrealism and Design*, ed. Ghislaine Wood (London: Victoria & Albert Museum, 2007), 53.

misbehaving puppy has just chewed it down raw, mistaking the coat rack for a toy.[37] Both Casey's and Reaves's pieces animate commonplace objects of the home through animality, an exercise of analogy that depends on fantasy rather than pure function: the vessels no longer only serve as containers but act as owls; the coat rack embraces dual identities as a *dog toy* and a *coat rack*. *Purple Conversation* and *Dog's Toy Coat Rack* stand next to each other in the exhibition at the ICA as two agents of animality.

The way Casey and Reaves couple animality with decorative and domestic objects recalls Surrealist transgressions between the organic and inorganic as well as animal and object. Emerging as an artistic movement in Paris of the 1920s, Surrealism traded in almost everything modernists had abandoned.[38] Fantasy and desire, symbolism and sensuous surfaces served as the motor of much Surrealist thought and practice, putting pressure on the coherence and control of the human subject's rational mind and relationship to the world.[39] By the 1930s, Surrealism entered a commercial phase, with artists directly tied to fashion, design, and other enterprises outside of fine art.[40] Méret Oppenheim's sculpture *Table with Bird's Feet*, 1938–39, for instance, not only hovers between sculpture and furniture, but it also combines avian imagery with domestic design (fig. 19). This hybrid work has its roots in Oppenheim's earlier sculptures, such as *Object*, 1935, a teacup, saucer, and spoon covered in fur. As a woman in a largely male artistic circle, Oppenheim imbues her sculpture with an erotic charge through the soft texture of animal fur, echoing the haptic expressions that tether Casey's and Reaves's practices together: the red hat and blue scarf in Casey's aptly titled *Hat and Scarf*, 2015, the silk fabric hugging Reaves's *Night Cabinet (Little Miss Attitude)*, 2016, like a tight dress, the disembodied hand caressing clay in Casey's *Pressing Matter*, 2015, and the

37 Reaves, conversation with the author, March 31, 2017.

38 Le Corbusier famously engaged in a war of words with Surrealist André Breton (although, ironically, the former incorporated Surrealist elements into his design for Carlos de Beistegui's apartment on the Champs-Elysées). For more information, see Anthony Vidler, "Home for Cyborgs," in *Not at Home: The Suppression of Domesticity in Modern Art andArchitecture*, ed. Christopher Reed (London: Thames and Hudson, 1996), 163; Wood, "The Illusory Interior," 54-56.

39 Igomen Racz, *Art and the Home: Comfort, Alienation, and the Everyday* (London: I.B. Tauris, 2015), 82-83; Anthony Vidler, *The Architectural Uncanny: Essays in the Modern Unhomely* (Cambridge, MA: The MIT Press, 1992), 150-53.

40 Ghislaine Wood, "Surreal Things: Making the 'fantastic real,'" in in *Surreal Things: Surrealism and Design*, ed. Ghislaine Wood (London: Victoria & Albert Museum, 2007), 2-6; Ulrich Lehmann, "The Uncommon Object: Surrealist Concepts and Categories for the Material World," in *Surreal Things: Surrealism and Design*, 19.

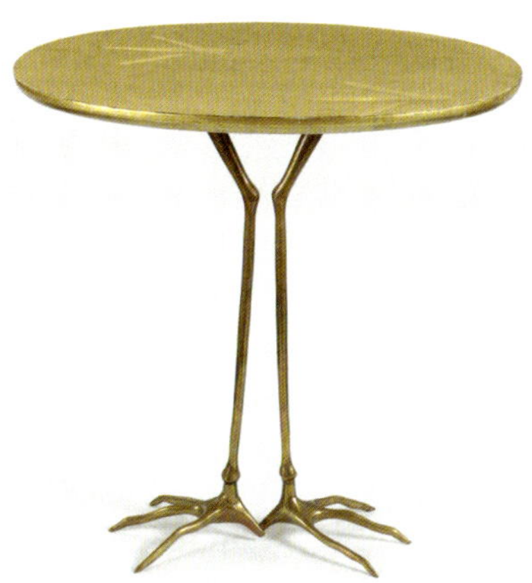

19
Méret Oppenheim, *Table with Bird's Legs*, 1938-39.
Made by Simon International, possibly in Italy, 1972-84.

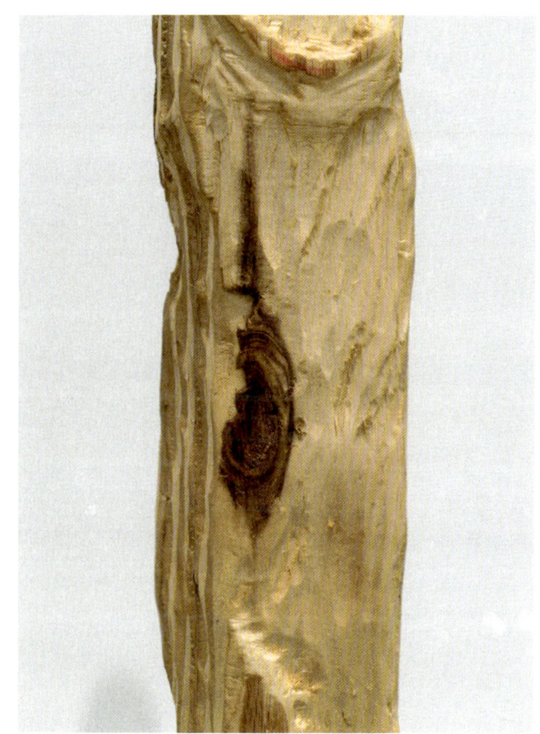

18
Jessi Reaves, *Dog's Toy Coat Rack*, detail, 2015
Canadian oak, steel, and varnish, 74 × 14¼ × 14.25 in

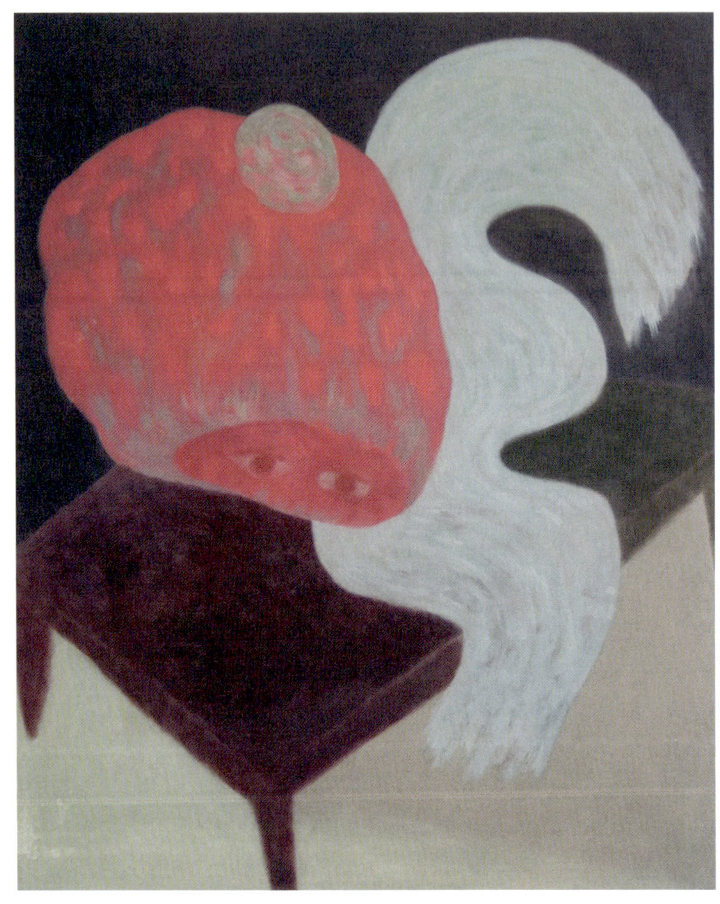

20
Ginny Casey, *Hat and Scarf*, 2015
Oil on canvas, 24 × 20 in.

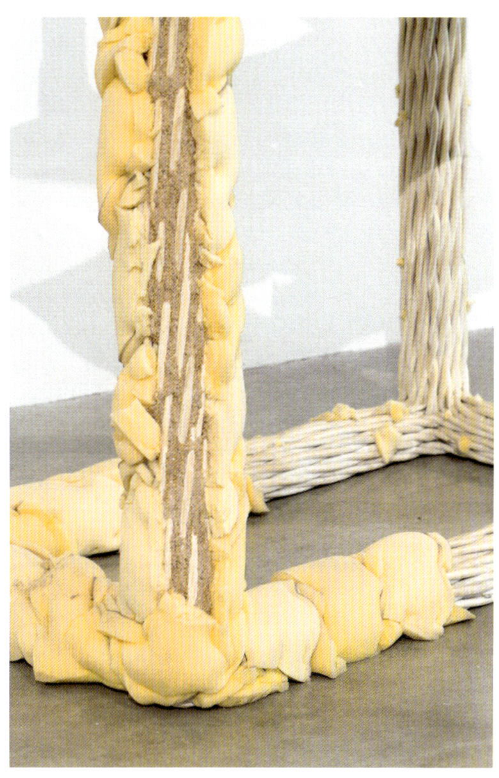

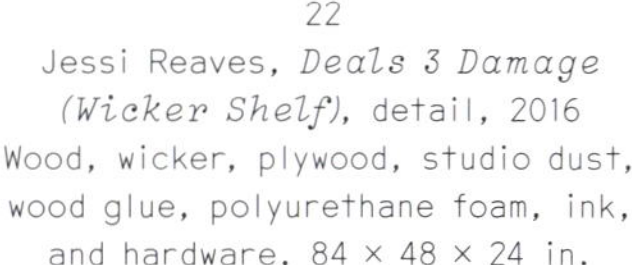

22
Jessi Reaves, *Deals 3 Damage (Wicker Shelf)*, detail, 2016
Wood, wicker, plywood, studio dust, wood glue, polyurethane foam, ink, and hardware, 84 × 48 × 24 in.

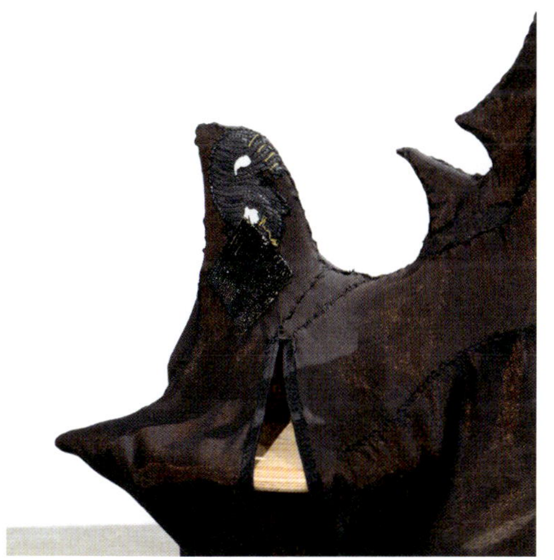

21
Jessi Reaves, *Night Cabinet (Little Miss Attitude)*, detail, 2016
Plywood, wood, steel, silk, and zippers, 72 × 32 × 26 in.

incongruous collision of wood, wicker, plywood, polyurethane and studio dust in Reaves's *Deals 3 Damage (Wicker Shelf)*, 2016 (figs. 20, 21, 22).[41]

In addition to animality, Surrealist artist and designers invoked a more generalized natural language of biomorphic curves and rounded shapes, inspired by Art Nouveau's turn-of-the-century union of the man-made and organic worlds, a particular target of Loos's diatribe against ornament.[42] Casey's inventory of vessels and small sculptures of all sizes, colors, and curves echoes Surrealist ceramics, such as the bulging vase in *Blue Vase with Ladder*, 2016, or the stack of rounded shapes in *Balancing Act*, 2017 (fig. 23). Even square and rectangular objects are given uneven edges and almost cartoonish profiles, from the peaks and crevices of the seesaw's perimeter in *Balancing Act* to the wonky legs of the table in *Moody Blue Studio*, 2017. The curves, curls, and other Baroque flourishes of Reaves's wooden wall shelves likewise adopt an exaggerated biomorphic logic. Reaves's *Noguchi Knockoff* series directly appeals to the biomorphic imaginary of midcentury modernism's own nod to Surrealism (fig. 24). What she knocks off is the iconic table by artist and designer Isamu Noguchi, whose dual allegiance to Surrealism and Modernism influenced his sculptural practice and furniture production. Working in the United States during the postwar period, Noguchi and others in his milieu rounded and softened the straight lines, sharp edges, and industrial materials inherited from Europe with curves, craft-like qualities, and natural materials.[43] Reaves takes Noguchi's biomorphic bent even further, swapping the smooth wooden base of the original for decidedly less graceful and yet more decorative organic materials such as sawdust and wood chips. The irreverent humor of her titles drives a wedge between Noguchi's natural sources and the table's mass production, itself a contradiction, given the fact that his work ended up furnishing many corporate offices across America during

41 Racz, *Art and the Home*, 83-84, 86; Robert Pincus-Warren, "The Furniture Paradigm," in *Improbable Furniture* (Philadelphia: University of Pennsylvania, 1977), 9-10.

42 Vidler, *The Architectural Uncanny*, 151, 153; Vidler, "Home for Cyborgs," 163, 167; Wood, "The Illusory Interior," 52; Foster, *Design and Crime*, 14-15; Bruderlin, "Introduction: Interior Exterior," 71; Ghislaine Wood, "The Shapes of Life: Biomorphism and American Design," in *Surreal Things: Surrealism and Design*, ed. Ghislaine Wood (London: Victoria & Albert Museum, 2007), 81-82.

43 Wood, "The Shapes of Life," 91-97; Gura, *Design After Modernism*, 23; Lowery Stokes Sims, "Rothko and the Four Seasons Commission: A Parable of Art and Design at Mid-Twentieth Century," in *Crafting Modernisms: Midcentury American Art and Design*, ed. Jeannine Falino (New York: Abrams, 2011), 60-61; Sparke; *The Modern Interior*, 188-89.

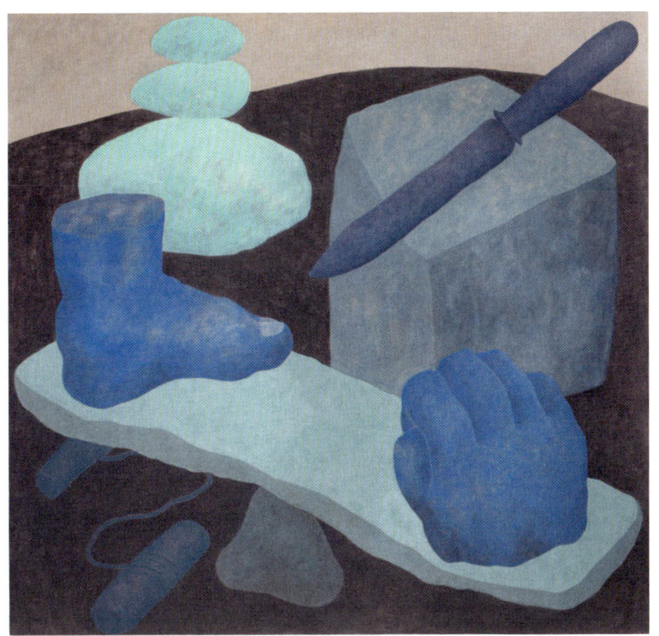

23
Ginny Casey, *Balancing Act*, 2017
Oil on canvas, 70 × 75 in.

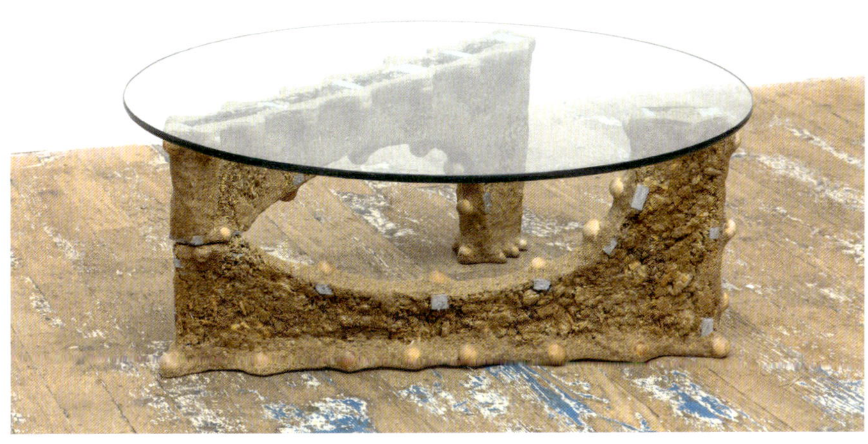

24
Jessi Reaves, *Quick-To-Sew Jester's Hat (Noguchi Knockoff #1)*, 2016
Cedar chips, sawdust, wood, glass, and pewter paint, 15 × 40 inches.

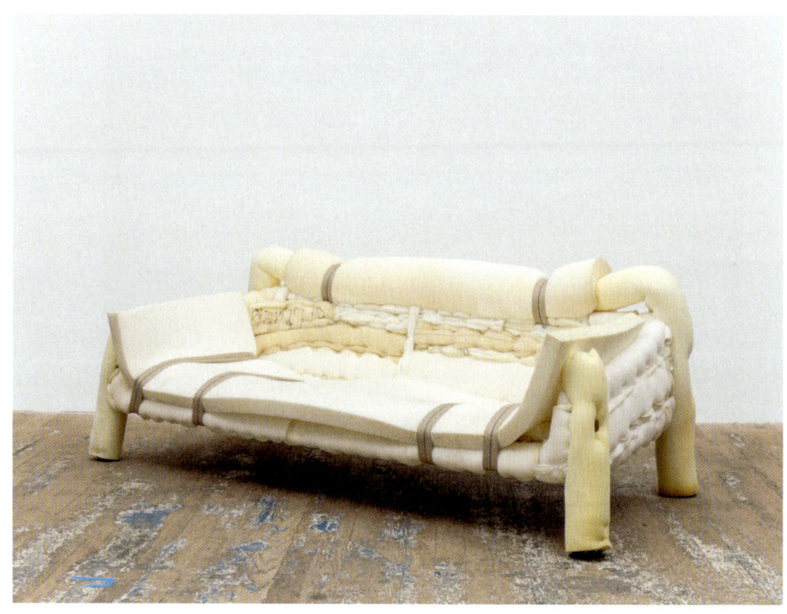

25
Jessi Reaves, *Foam Couch with Straps*, 2016
Upholstery foam, fiberglass,
wood, and webbing, 29 × 77 × 35 in.

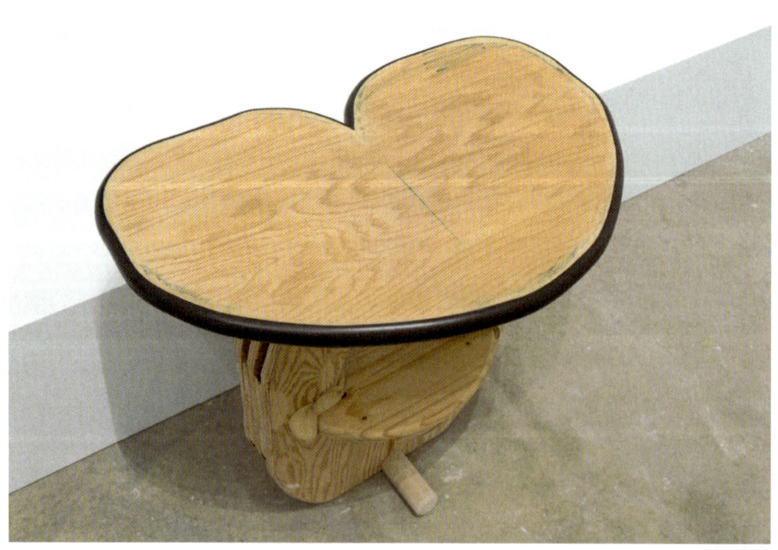

26
Jessi Reaves, *Smushed Butt Table*, 2016
Plywood, pine, rubber, polyurethane
foam, plastic, and ink, 30 × 30 × 28 in.

the postwar economic boom.[44] Reaves, in turn, offers a chunkier, rougher "knockoff," a kitschy cousin produced in multiples yet handmade in her studio.

While animal and organic imagery mark both Casey's and Reaves's work, each artist also attaches anthropomorphic elements to their deceptively ordinary objects. Reaves's *Foam Couch with Straps*, 2016, sags and bulges like an aging body, weary from the burdens life so often brings (fig. 25). The artist's *Smushed Butt Table*, 2016, gets to this point most directly (fig. 26). The top of the simple plywood and pine table assumes the shape of a "smushed butt," making a mockery of, in some sense, the inviolability of the line between inanimate and animate, object and subject, furniture and the people who rely upon these quotidian structures, like a table, every day. Its form, moreover, refuses to just follow function, taking up the rather fanciful idea that a table and a "smushed butt" might have something in common. Salvador Dalí and Edward James's *Mae West Lips Sofa*, 1936, similarly partakes of the Surrealist concern of fragmented human anatomy, uncanny objecthood, and domestic furniture. Plush and pink, the sofa assumes the shape of a woman's lips at an overblown scale, two of which framed the fireplace in the dining room at Monkton House, James's home in Sussex, England.[45] It derives from Dalí's earlier work *Mae West's Face which May Be Used as a Surrealist Apartment*, 1934–35, a representation of an interior mapped onto a celebrity's countenance: her eyes have become paintings, her hair a surrogate for heavy drapery, and her lips a soft sofa (fig. 27).[46] Several decades later, Dalí revisited the actress's face, partnering with architect Oscar Tusquets Blanca to conceive of *Mae West Room*, c. 1974, in the Dalí Theatre-Museum (fig. 28). Based on *Mae West's Face which May Be Used as a Surrealist Apartment*, the later installation takes the apartment part of the two-dimensional original quite literally, translating the domestic space pictured in the early work into a three-dimensional room. In these and other of Dalí's

44 Jeremy Myerson, "After modernism: the contemporary office environment," in *Interior Design and Identity*, eds. Susie McKellar and Penny Sparke (Manchester: Manchester University Press, 2004), 193-94; Marcus, *Functionalist Design*, 127, 145; Sparke, *The Modern Interior*, 188-92.

45 Wood, "The Illusory Interior," 49, 52-53.

46 Ibid., 40-42.

works, the decorative aspects of the home—curtains, paintings, and sofas—are ripe for Surrealist forms of estrangement and metamorphosis, while the human body also lends itself to the force of the domestic uncanny.

Dalí's various manifestations of Mae West's face dramatize how the artist's Surrealist imagination suspends the two- and three-dimensional, representational and real, painting and sculpture, within an uncanny orbit of anthropomorphic decoration and furniture. The paintings of Casey and the sculptures of Reaves inhabit this supple space as well. If Reaves's table resembles a smushed butt, then the severed hands, feet, fingers, and ears populating Casey's paintings undergo a process of calcification, thingly and eerie in fragmented form. To be sure, many of the domestic things in Casey's painted world acquire human characteristics, such as the purple vase standing akimbo in *Fan with Jugs*, 2017, or the semi-abstract, semi-lifelike figures in mid-conversation in *Chatty Forms*, 2016 (fig. 29). But more often than not, Casey subjects human body parts to objectification, like a sculptor turning raw matter into recognizable form or a potter molding a vessel on the wheel. In *The Potter's Ear*, 2015, for instance, the titular organ floats underneath a chunky vase presumably thrown by an unseen potter, whose tools lie on the table. Casey treats the ear as equivalent to any other seemingly inanimate object in the same picture plane. Moreover, the deliberate appearance of these instruments of handcrafted labor across several paintings signals a human presence that nevertheless remains largely absent from scenes where objects, rather than people, take center stage. Casey's small studies further implicate the act of making through the easily collectable—even cute—size of preparatory work. Although the studies provide windows into the artist's process in all its unfinished scratchiness, they avoid privileging it as raw evidence of Casey's hand and subjective experience. Rather, despite their modest scale, the studies still provide ample room for

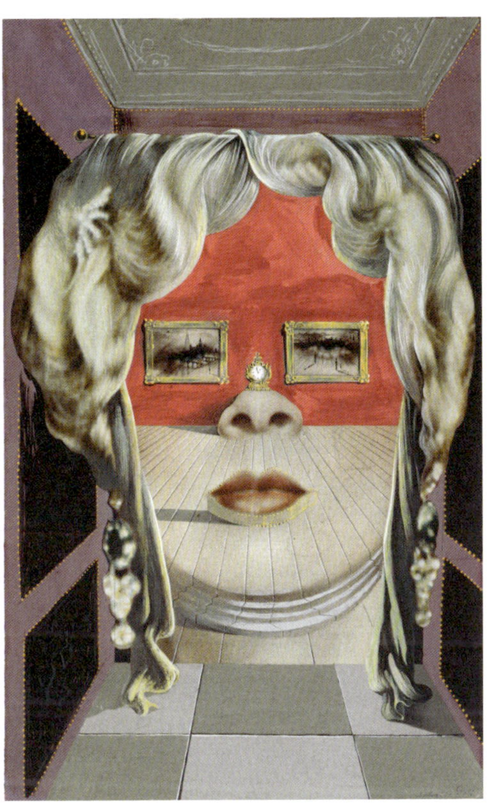

27
Salvador Dalí, *Mae West's Face which May be Used as a Surrealist Apartment*, 1934-35
Gouache with graphite, on commercially printed magazine page, 11 × 7 in.

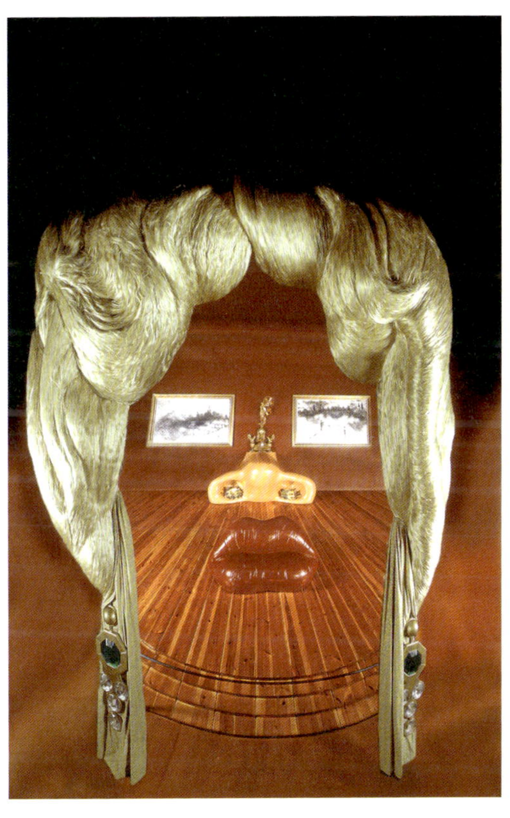

28
Salvador Dalí and Oscar Tusquets Blanca, *Mae West Room*, c. 1974
Installation.

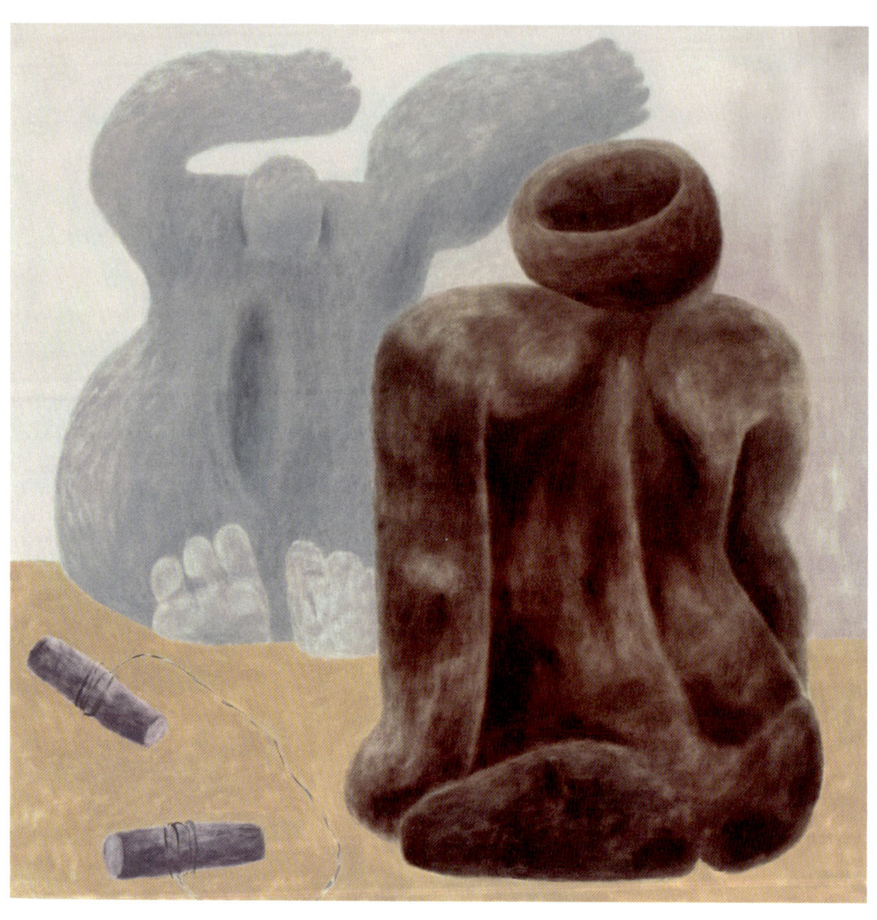

29
Ginny Casey, *Chatty Forms*, 2016
Oil on canvas, 30 × 30 in.

ordinary objects to engage and sometimes misbehave against or beyond the limits imposed by function.

"This chair will have life," Dalí once noted on a design for an armchair. "It will breathe." Although Dalí never realized this particular piece, he did design "fantastical furniture" for his own apartment in Paris.[47] The "fantastical" forms of domestic objects rebuts not only the rational functionalism espoused by his contemporaries in modern design circles, but this unexpected animacy indexes Surrealism's fascination with Sigmund Freud's theory of the uncanny. In a 1919 essay, Freud described the uncanny as the strange or unfamiliar in the deeply familiar, such as the home. For Freud, the domestic interior no longer just signified the comfort of familial bliss. It could also contain erotic energies and desires, nightmares and dreams; in short, the interiority of our own unconscious beyond the purview of conscious control.[48] The body and symbol of woman often served as the ground on which artists and designers elaborated the irrational interior, such as Dalí's obsession with Mae West's face. This trope repeated and extended the notion of a woman's place in the home as a part-object among many others.[49] At the same time, this vision of "domesticity and its discontents" presented a psychic space for female artists and designers, such as Oppenheim, to undermine inherited ideologies around the home, and, in particular, the woman's place in or outside of it.[50]

Casey's strange scenes of interior spaces and Reaves's equally wild and weird furniture-*cum*-sculpture approach the home as a site of investigation and experimentation, excursions into the uncanny wilderness of everyday life rather than simply a source of the status quo. In some cases, this results in objects marked by gender. Casey's rounded vessels might evoke the age-old equation of women's bodies with vases and other curved containers, particularly given the fact that the artist,

47 Dalí, quoted in Wood, "The Illusory Interior," 53.

48 Racz, *Art and the Home*, 85; Wood, "The Illusory Interior," 40, 49; Vidler, *The Architectural Uncanny*, x-xi, 14; Rice, *The Emergence of the Interior*, 39-40.

49 Wood, "Surreal Things," 10.

50 Vidler, *The Architectural Uncanny*, x; Racz, *Art and Home*, 83-84; Wood, "The Illusory Interior," 12.

as she has noted herself, was pregnant when painting much of this work. Yet she also denies us the easy pleasure of this idealized reading, and in fact recalibrates domestic stuff and space toward the surreal and scary, even to scenes of destruction. The vessels are oversize, intimidating in their stature in the small studies as well. Vases are both preserved and shattered in *Blue Vase with Ladder*, while raw matter itself is either lovingly caressed or disturbingly crushed in *Pressing Matter*. The containers in *Fan with Jugs* seem to possess distinct personalities or temperaments, confident in their size, color, and posture. Reaves, for one, gives *Night Cabinet (Little Miss Attitude)* a feminine epithet, an imposing piece with spiked edges and other qualities befitting its title. Both artists materialize Loos's "nightmares" or Greenberg's "specters" of domestic decoration that chafe against mutually reinforcing norms of femininity and domesticity.

In several of the works, strangeness assumes the form of an alien or cyborg presence. Reaves's *Mutant Butterfly Chair*, 2017, transforms a familiar modern design into its mutant offspring by using a rich maroon-colored leather for the seat decorated with a cut-out of a butterfly and by affixing bulbous shapes to the base construction. Casey uses scale to disrupt our habitual sense of space and self with something stranger. An overgrown metronome faces off against a smaller, lime-green armchair in *Keeping Time*, as if some mad scientist has turned this musical machine into a cyborg, let loose to terrorize other objects in the home. Once again, another iconic Surrealist sculpture reverberates with Casey's mutant metronome. Man Ray's *Indestructible Object (or Object to be Destroyed)*, 1964 (replica of 1934 original), a metronome with a cut-out image of the eye of the artist's former partner and assistant Lee Miller, suggests questions of violence, everyday objects, anthropomorphism, and the female body that run like a red thread throughout Casey's

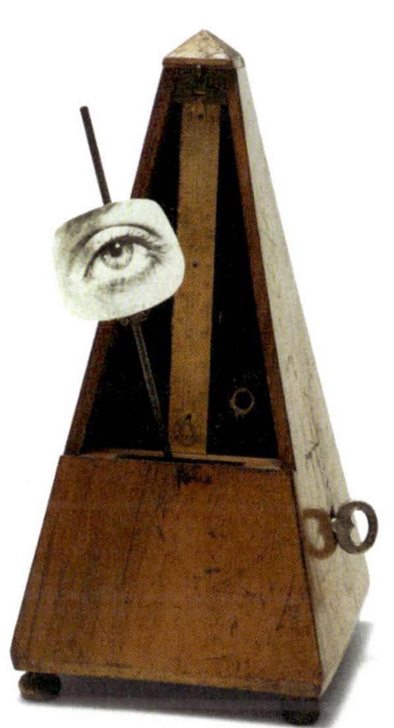

30
Man Ray, *Indestructible Object (or Object to Be Destroyed)*, 1964 (replica of 1923 original)
Metronome with cutout photograph of eye on pendulum, 8⅞ × 4⅜ × 4⅝ in.

paintings as well (fig. 30).[51] The overstuffed green chair in this painting echoes Reaves's equally overstuffed green, yellow, and tan armchair and ottoman, *Idol of the Hares*, 2014 (fig. 31). Bursting at the seams, *Idol of the Hares* cuts an odd if not striking figure with its mix of colors, extensive stitching, and enormous appendages, a mystical being or "idol" masquerading as furniture. Moving from interiority to interior spaces, Casey's and Reaves's simultaneously ordinary and altogether animated chairs, vases, and cabinets recover the fantasies and fears in the Surrealist encounter between human, very often female, subject and domestic object.

"Four quaint small rooms," or Ottomans and Ornament[52]

"Enter the museum bench," write Diana Fuss and Joel Sanders, "a nearly ubiquitous but frequently disparaged piece of furniture, as routinely overlooked as it is regularly used."[53] In their essay "An Aesthetic Headache: Notes from the Museum Bench," Fuss and Sanders trace the evolution of the museum bench: from a plush spot on which to look *and* linger in comfort to a spare seat that ignores the needs of the viewer's body, made to be as inconspicuous as possible in today's museum. This shift reflects a larger change in the function of museums as a social site for multiple activities to the museum as a quasi-sacred space, a temple of art for purely optical and "individual" spectatorship.[54] "Exactly why has the museum bench become an object of curatorial, critical, and cultural disdain?" the authors ask. "The bench's very presence, when acknowledged, reminds us that the act of spectatorship may not be nearly as disembodied, nor the gallery space nearly as neutral, as we still commonly assume."[55] The bench also serves as a worthy reminder of our dependence on domestic objects,

51 One of the originals, entitled *Object to Be Destroyed*, was in fact destroyed by Parisian students in 1957; as a rejoinder, Man Ray made many replicas, insuring the difficulty of total destruction, hence the new title, *Indestructible Object*. For more information, see the Museum of Modern Art website, "Indestructible Object (or Object to be Destroyed," accessed May 22, 2017, www.moma.org/learn/moma_learning/man-ray-indestructible-object-1964-replica-of-1923-original.

52 Katherine Dreier, quoted in Meyer, "Big, Middle-Class Modernism," 99.

53 Diana Fuss and Joel Sanders, "An Aesthetic Headache: Notes from the Museum Bench," in *Interiors: CCS Readers: Perspectives on Art and Culture*, eds. Johanna Burton, Lynne Cooke, and Josiah McElheny (Annandale-on-Hudson, NY: Center for Curatorial Studies, Bard College/Sternberg Press, 2012), 65.

54 Ibid., 65–71.

55 Ibid., 66.

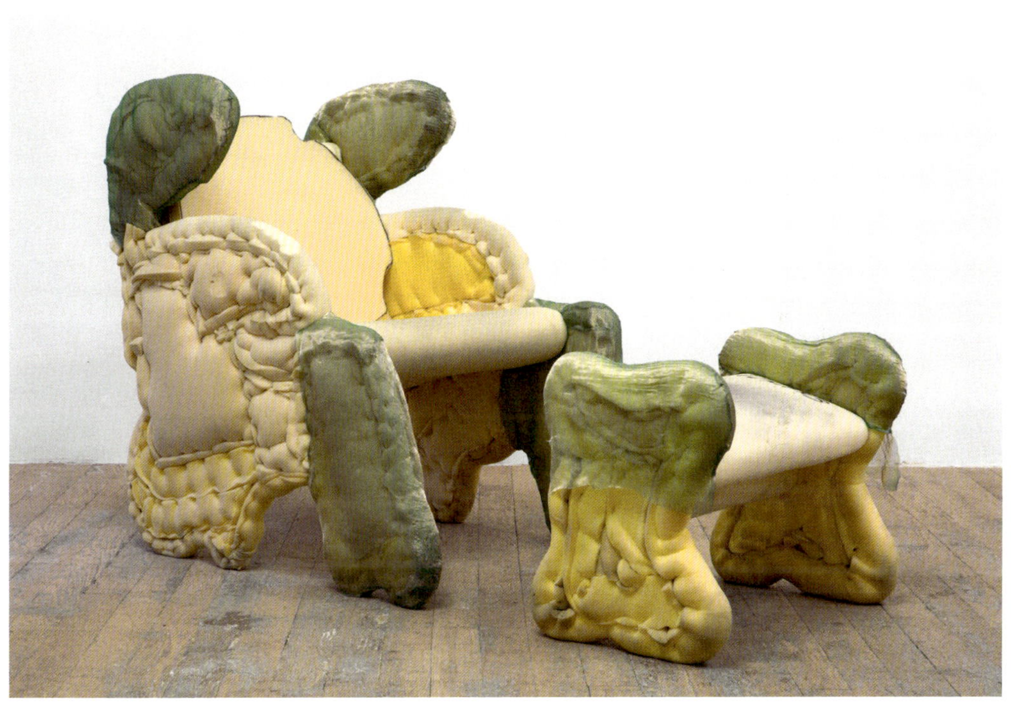

31
Jessi Reaves, *Idol of the Hares*, 2014
Oak, polyurethane foam, silk, cotton,
aluminum, and ink, 38 × 28 × 48 in.

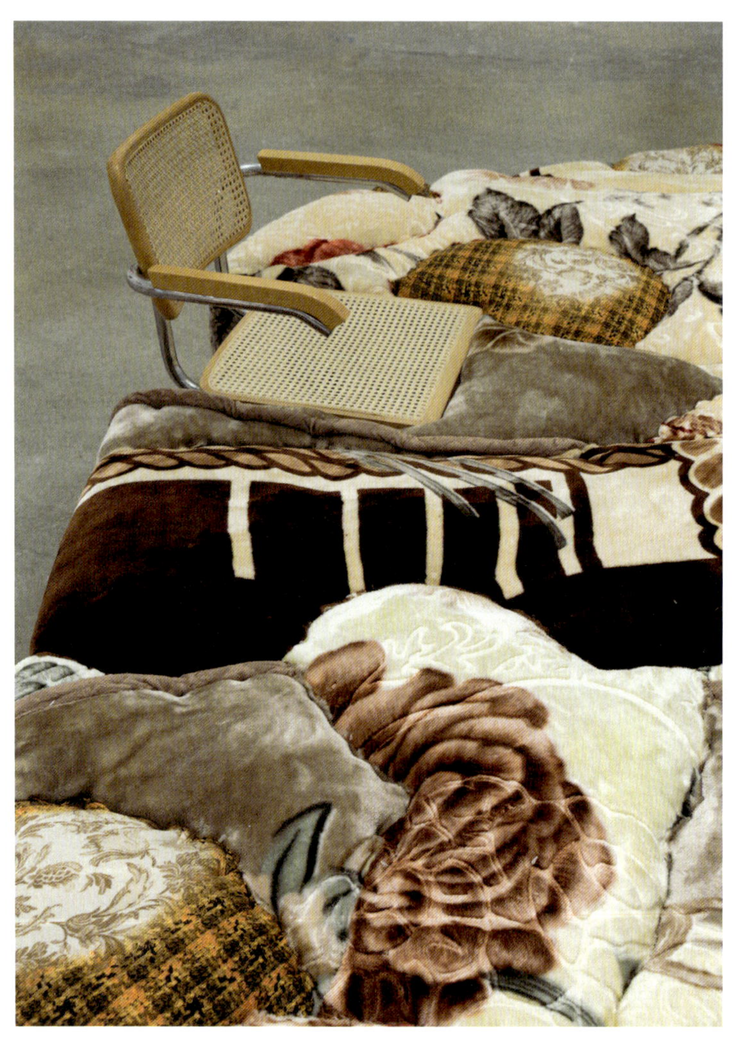

32
Jessi Reaves, *Ottoman with Parked Chair & Ottoman*, detail, 2017
Plywood, foam, fleece, fabric, hardware, and found furniture, 130 × 111 × 19 in.

even in public space. As Fuss and Sanders point out, the bench brings viewers back and down, grounding us in our body and alerting us to our corporeal limits. An act of "submission" and "not sovereignty," these postures of reliance carry "the taint of femininity and domesticity" traditionally excised from the history of both modernism and the museum.[56]

Unlike the unwelcoming seating often found in museum galleries, Reaves's objects remain generous to their users. The artist deliberately makes her work comfortable, which in part accounts for the foam and other varieties of soft surfaces that adorn her functional sculptures. *Ottoman with Parked Chair & Ottoman*, 2017, conceived specifically for the exhibition at the ICA, invites viewers to take a seat and stay awhile (fig. 32). Upholstered with velvety blankets, the large ottoman wraps around the short edge of a wall and faces a platform displaying Casey's paintings and *Kragel's Nap Chair*. Since the ottoman provides ample space to lie down and can accommodate several people at once, it validates spectatorship as the doubly corporeal and social experience it once was. Embedded within this ottoman are another B64 and a small Thonet ottoman. The contrast between these smaller pieces and the larger upholstered ottoman can quite literally be felt: the found furniture's unembellished surfaces of bent wood, steel, and chair cane or the ottoman's plush blankets with a rosy floral pattern that decorates the entire piece with a homespun femininity and even endearing gaudiness. The material insurgence of the ottoman prompts the material reality of spectatorship—the body behind our eyes or the fatigue of our frames, our desire for conversation or coziness. *Ottoman with Parked Chair & Ottoman* ushers in prior histories of the museum bench before its sensual surfaces, decorative fabrics, and social sites were purged as embarrassing relics of the dependent body, the domestic, and the feminine.

56 Ibid., 75–76.

Reaves's seating in the exhibition enjoys multiple states as artworks and surrogate museum benches. In so doing, they quickly disarm viewers of ingrained habits of viewing and museum decorum: don't touch the artwork, use only your eyes. As a site to view many of Casey's paintings that feature hands, fingers, and other haptic elements, Reaves's sculptures perform within a larger field of textured relations that includes viewers as well. And when in the company of Reaves's furniture, Casey's paintings here function as art and ornament across from the chair or catty-corner to the shelf or next to the chaise—singular paintings *and* one part of what could be a larger domestic decorative schema, department-store vignette, or even theatrical set. This installation jettisons modes of display that celebrate the autonomy of easel paintings or sculptures on pedestals, divorced from the world around. The twiggy nature of Reaves's *Dog's Toy Coat Rack*, for example, reverberates with the branch in Casey's *Purple Conversation*; the spiky edges of *Night Cabinet (Little Miss Attitude)* are reminiscent of the crook of the vessel's elbow in the nearby canvas, *Fan with Jugs*; the brownish-red color palette of *Mutant Butterfly Chair* is picked up in *Moody Blue Studio*, the painting across from the chair; and the butts in *Chatty Forms* resemble the shape of the surface in *Smushed Butt Table*, which is in fact smushed against the platform on which the painting is displayed. The arrangement on and around the platform itself both nods to and upends the way conventions of design display aspire for autonomy: neat lines of chairs, for example, positioned on pristine platforms and insulated from context. *This* platform, however, deliberately mixes type and media—art, design, and something in between. *Kragel's Nap Chair* sits next to three paintings by Casey. Two canvases casually lean against the wall, evoking a homier space and its more haphazard hangings. The aforementioned table breaks rules of museum display, stubbornly sitting flush against the platform rather than at a comfortable distance from it. Reaves's *Worthless Lump (Lamp)*, 2017, a fully functional standing lamp, arcs over *Kragel's Nap Chair*, ready to light the page for an anticipated reader. This installation—and the works in it—refuse isolation for contingency, dependency, and relationality, fundamental to the exhibition design and viewing experience.

Modern painting has distinguished itself from decoration by clinging to this very notion of independence from environment.[57] And yet the history of modernism in the museum has in many ways pointed to the fiction of this asocial condition precisely through the language of domestic decoration.[58] Even Le Corbusier's Pavillon L'Esprit Nouveau represented a model home where paintings, no matter how purist, decorated the walls, and furniture was meant to be used. Moreover, many collecting and display practices of women transgressed the boundary between art and life, public and private, from the most casual in the home to foundational hangings of modern art.[59] As part of her work in the *Société Anonyme*, the great art patron Katherine Dreier conceived of "four quaint small rooms" as modes of display for the 1926–27 *International Exhibition of Modern Art* at the Brooklyn Museum (fig. 33). The rooms—a parlor, a dining room, a library, and a bedroom—showcased modern art alongside more traditional wooden furniture, urns, and other items, a decorative schema borrowed from her own home. By purchasing furniture from a local department store for the exhibition, Dreier also borrows from the logic of retail displays that purposefully mimes domestic space.[60] This exchange has also been reversed. Architect, designer, and collector Pierre Chareau, for instance, designed a study for a 1928 exhibition on French decorative arts at Lord & Taylor in New York, where his iconic sconces hung on the walls near a painting and

57 Troy, "Domesticity, Decoration and Consumer Culture," 114-11; Molesworth, "Louise Lawler," 21.

58 There are an abundance of historical moments when commercial and domestic modes of display influenced or infiltrated museums devoted to modern art and design—too many to address in this short essay. Two other noteworthy examples include MoMA's *House in the Museum Garden* series, which featured one by Breuer in 1949, as well as the Walker Art Center's *Idea House*, first exhibited in 1941. For more information, see Joachim Driller, "On Houses and Palaces: Remarks on Marcel Breuer's Residential Houses," in *Marcel Breuer: Design and Architecture* (Weil am Rhein: Vitra Design Museum, 2003), 218; Alexandra Griffith Winton, "'A man's house is his art': Walker Art Center's Idea House project and the marketing of domestic design, 1941-7," in *The Modern Period Room: The Construction of the Exhibited Interior, 1870 to 1950*, eds. Penny Sparke, Brenda Martin, and Trevor Keeble (London; New York: Routledge, 2006), 87-88.

59 Molesworth, "Louise Lawler," 20.

60 Meyer, "Big, Middle-Class Modernism," 78, 99-101, 112.

watercolors by Fernand Léger and a drawing by Pablo Picasso, to name but a few artworks in rotation (fig. 34).[61] These exhibitions mark moments when art meets life, sometimes in all its crass commercialism, and provide a distant but significant historical backdrop for how *Ginny Casey & Jessi Reaves* improvises on intertwined histories of commercial, domestic, and museum displays.

Former homes have often served as spaces for museums or galleries, such as the second location of the Museum of Modern Art, a nineteenth-century brownstone. This building held Philip Johnson's famed 1934 exhibition *Machine Art*, which showcased utilitarian, machine-made design objects, from kitchenware to scientific laboratory equipment. Johnson famously covered the decorative moldings of the building to match the spare aesthetic of the design on display. Johnson's erasure of the building's ornamental residues of Victorian-era domesticity underscores the antagonism between modern design and domestic decoration.[62] Still, decoration here remains the "specter that haunts modernism"; its erasure calls attention to its absence, just behind Johnson's purposeful obstructions. Casey has also shown her paintings in a former townhouse; but instead of covering the decorative aspects of the building, her variously sized canvases feel right at home in the intimate space of Half Gallery on the Upper East Side of New York, where many of these homes-*cum*-galleries still reside (fig. 35). The moldings on the ceiling and fireplace echo the ornamental curves of the chair and table in nearby *Blue Table*, and the smaller size and lower ceilings of the rooms contribute an aura of intimacy, as if the viewer just walked into someone's apartment, decorated with paintings. The fireplace, crown molding, and built-in bookshelf at Half Gallery contrast with what in many ways has become the standard for exhibition spaces: bare white walls enclosing vacuous spaces cleaned of physical or affective particularity. Reesa Greenberg identifies a change beginning in the 1960s from the display of art in

61 Esther da Costa Meyer, "Pierre Chareau: A Life Interrupted," in Esther da Costa Meyer, *Pierre Chareau: Modern Architecture and Design* (New Haven: Yale University Press, 2016), 25.

62 The Museum of Modern Art website, "Machine Art: March 5–April 29, 1934: The Museum of Modern Art," accessed April 11, 2017, www.moma.org/calendar/exhibitions/1784.

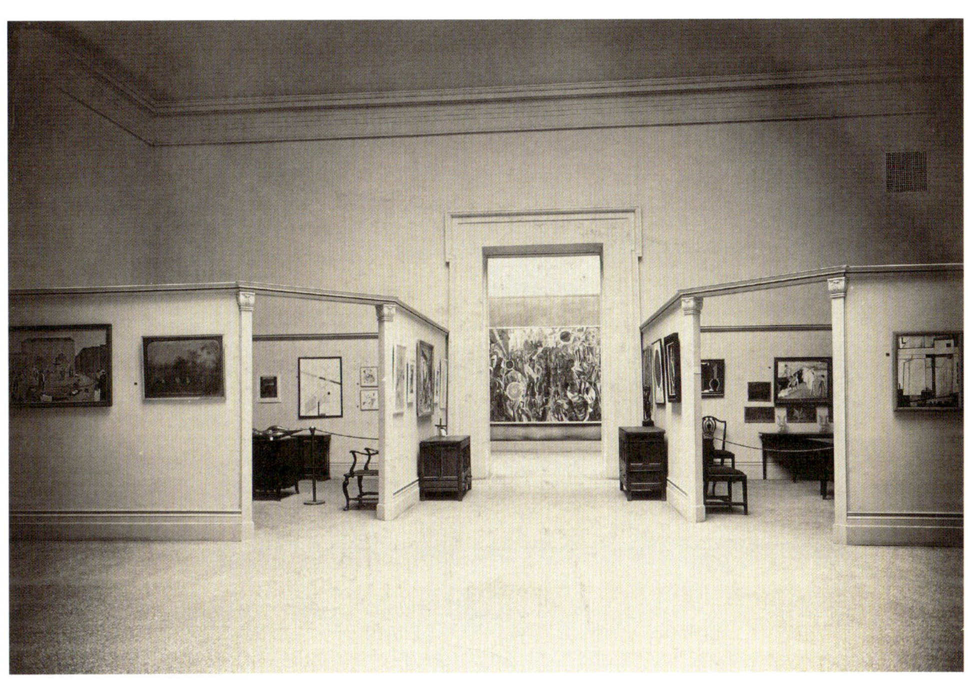

33
International Exhibition of Modern Art, 1926-27,
installation view, Brooklyn Museum.

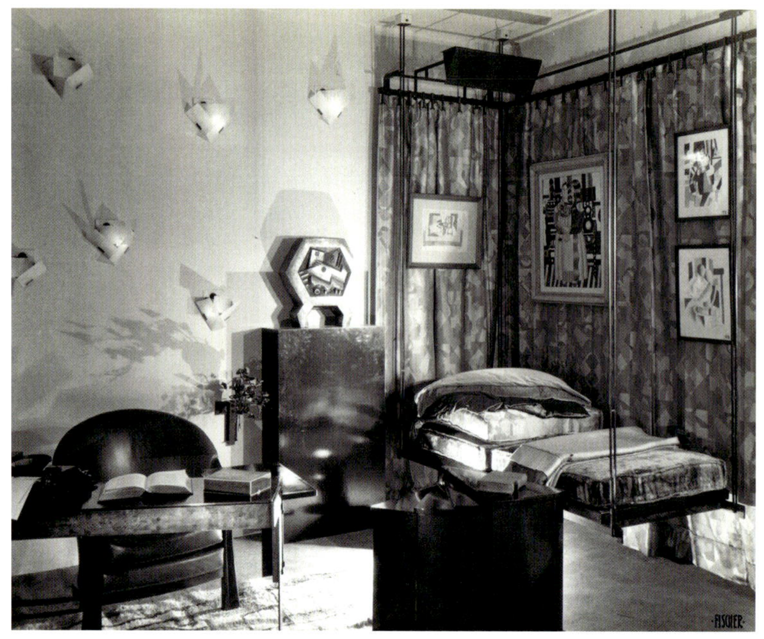

34
Study designed by Pierre Chareau for
an exhibition on French Decorative arts at
Lord and Taylor, New York, 1928.

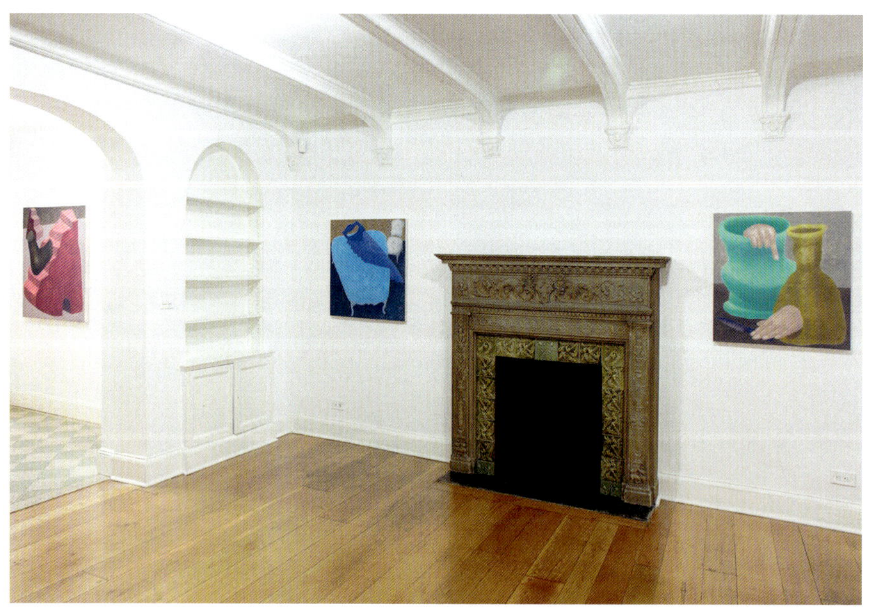

35
Play Things, 2016, installation view,
Half Gallery, New York.

homes with furniture to former warehouses or factories absent of seating, the domestic to industrial, the Upper East Side to Chelsea in New York. These larger venues could also hold increasingly monumental art, such as the heavy tectonics of Minimalist sculptures.[63] Although the concrete floors, high ceilings, and bare walls at the ICA appear more akin to an industrial aesthetic, the three walls in the middle of the exhibition create smaller and more hospitable areas. Reaves's sculptures likewise never lose sight of human scale. And while Casey's paintings vary in size, she continually chooses to depict the home's humble object, no matter how strange it has become.

In 1977, the ICA opened *Improbable Furniture*, an exhibition that considered how furniture and design inform art (fig. 36).[64] It featured a range of artists, including Richard Artschwager, whose work brings together painting and sculpture through the *concept* of, rather than actual, furniture. Artschwager's *Description of a Table*, 1964, seen in the exhibition's installation shots represents the idea of a table. Through basic visual cues of a table's ontological condition, the artist stretches the two-dimensional image of a table into three dimensions, an illusion that "establishes an unsettling tension," according to Suzanne Delehanty's catalogue essay for the exhibition, "between surface and volume, between pictorial and sculptural form."[65] "I wanted to make a sculpture for the eye and a painting for the touch," noted the artist about his work.[66] Unlike Reaves's furniture-sculpture hybrids, Artschwager's "archetypes" of tables, chairs, and the like do not function as such.[67] Yet navigating the interstices of painting, sculpture, and furniture, Artschwager's work occasions a fundamental coexistence at the heart of *Ginny Casey & Jessi Reaves*, one that operates

63 Reesa Greenberg, "The Exhibition Redistributed: A Case for Reassessing Space," in *Thinking About Exhibitions*, eds. Reesa Greenberg, Bruce W. Ferguson, and Sandy Nairne (London; New York: Routledge, 1996), 350–52.

64 Pincus-Warren, "The Furniture Paradigm," 8.

65 Suzanne Delehanty, "Furniture of Another Order," in *Improbable Furniture* (Philadelphia: University of Pennsylvania, 1977), 26; Stokes Sims, "Rothko and the Four Seasons Commission," 63.

66 Richard Artschwager, quoted in Melitta Kliege, "Challenge to Looking: The Paintings and Sculptures of Richard Artschwager," in *Richard Artschwager: Up and Across* (Nürnberg: Verlag für moderne Kunst, 2001), 30.

67 Delehanty, "Furniture of Another Order," 26.

across boundaries among media but also public and private spaces, museum and home, familiar and strange.

The catalogue for *Improbable Furniture* also attends to the friction between modernism and Surrealism. The exhibition, too, includes work by Dalí and other Surrealists.[68] For Delehanty, furniture in some sense registers this tension as "the world we choose to call real and the world of our imagination."[69] These functional and fanciful worlds collide in the work of Casey and Reaves, where cabinets have attitude, vessels have conversations, and visitors have time and space to rest and recline on an artwork. *Ginny Casey & Jessi Reaves* insists on art's other life as decorative and domestic objects: used, loved, and lived with but also whimsical, weird, disobedient, desiring. Everyday and enchanted, Casey's paintings and Reaves's sculptures function as ordinary repositories of dreams, nightmares, and fantasies that are embedded within, rather than removed from, the fabric of the world.

68 Pincus-Warren, "The Furniture Paradigm," 8–10, 14; Delehanty, "Furniture of Another Order," 21–22.

69 Delehanty, "Furniture of Another Order," 20.

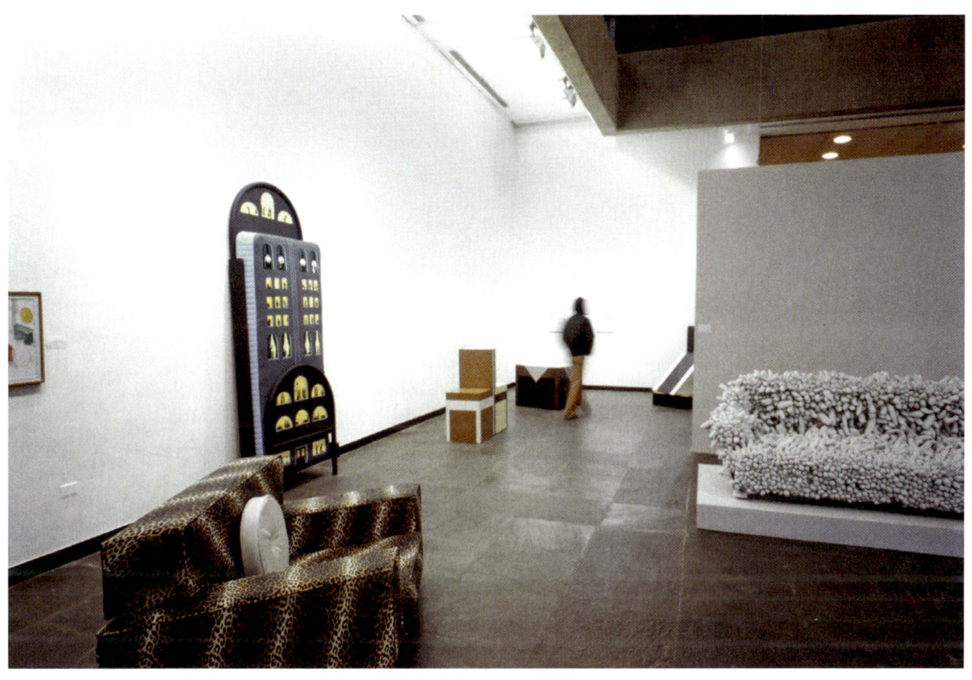

36
Improbable Furniture, 1977, installation view,
Institute of Contemporary Art, University of Pennsylvania, Philadelphia

Ginny Casey & Jessi Reaves

Institute of Contemporary Art
University of Pennsylvania, Philadelphia
April 28–August 6, 2017

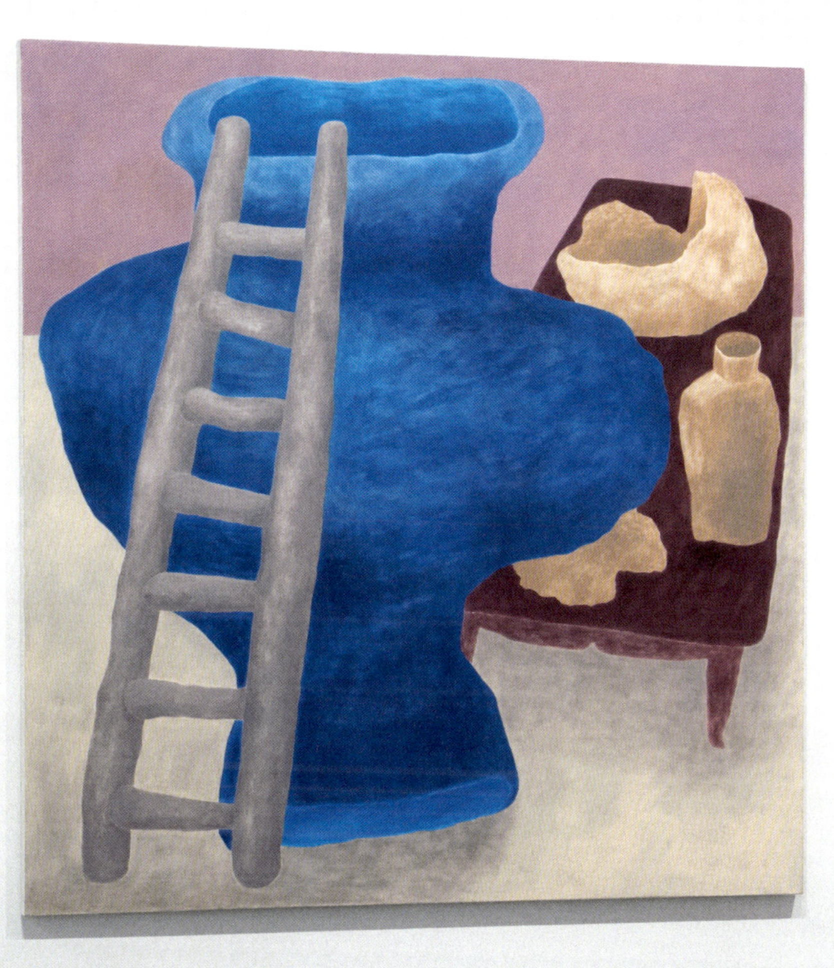

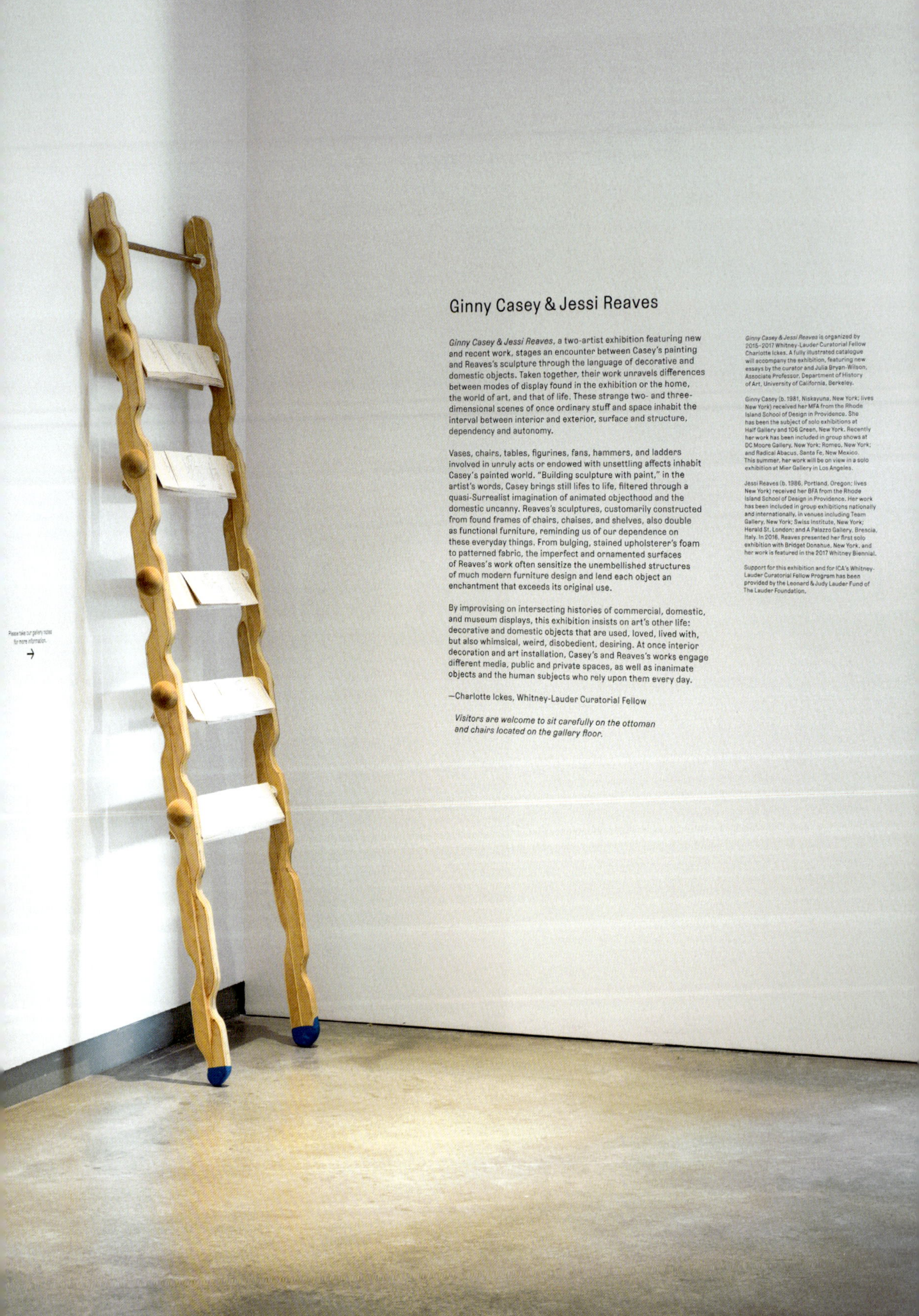
Please take our gallery notes for more information.
→
Ginny Casey & Jessi Reaves
Ginny Casey & Jessi Reaves, a two-artist exhibition featuring new and recent work, stages an encounter between Casey's painting and Reaves's sculpture through the language of decorative and domestic objects. Taken together, their work unravels differences between modes of display found in the exhibition or the home, the world of art, and that of life. These strange two- and three-dimensional scenes of once ordinary stuff and space inhabit the interval between interior and exterior, surface and structure, dependency and autonomy.
Vases, chairs, tables, figurines, fans, hammers, and ladders involved in unruly acts or endowed with unsettling affects inhabit Casey's painted world. "Building sculpture with paint," in the artist's words, Casey brings still lifes to life, filtered through a quasi-Surrealist imagination of animated objecthood and the domestic uncanny. Reaves's sculptures, customarily constructed from found frames of chairs, chaises, and shelves, also double as functional furniture, reminding us of our dependence on these everyday things. From bulging, stained upholsterer's foam to patterned fabric, the imperfect and ornamented surfaces of Reaves's work often sensitize the unembellished structures of much modern furniture design and lend each object an enchantment that exceeds its original use.
By improvising on intersecting histories of commercial, domestic, and museum displays, this exhibition insists on art's other life: decorative and domestic objects that are used, loved, lived with, but also whimsical, weird, disobedient, desiring. At once interior decoration and art installation, Casey's and Reaves's works engage different media, public and private spaces, as well as inanimate objects and the human subjects who rely upon them every day.
—Charlotte Ickes, Whitney-Lauder Curatorial Fellow
Visitors are welcome to sit carefully on the ottoman and chairs located on the gallery floor.
Ginny Casey & Jessi Reaves is organized by 2015–2017 Whitney-Lauder Curatorial Fellow Charlotte Ickes. A fully illustrated catalogue will accompany the exhibition, featuring new essays by the curator and Julia Bryan-Wilson, Associate Professor, Department of History of Art, University of California, Berkeley.
Ginny Casey (b. 1981, Niskayuna, New York; lives New York) received her MFA from the Rhode Island School of Design in Providence. She has been the subject of solo exhibitions at Half Gallery and 106 Green, New York. Recently her work has been included in group shows at DC Moore Gallery, New York; Romeo, New York; and Radical Abacus, Santa Fe, New Mexico. This summer, her work will be on view in a solo exhibition at Mier Gallery in Los Angeles.
Jessi Reaves (b. 1986, Portland, Oregon; lives New York) received her BFA from the Rhode Island School of Design in Providence. Her work has been included in group exhibitions nationally and internationally, in venues including Team Gallery, New York; Swiss Institute, New York; Herald St, London; and A Palazzo Gallery, Brescia, Italy. In 2016, Reaves presented her first solo exhibition with Bridget Donahue, New York, and her work is featured in the 2017 Whitney Biennial.
Support for this exhibition and for ICA's Whitney-Lauder Curatorial Fellow Program has been provided by the Leonard & Judy Lauder Fund of The Lauder Foundation.

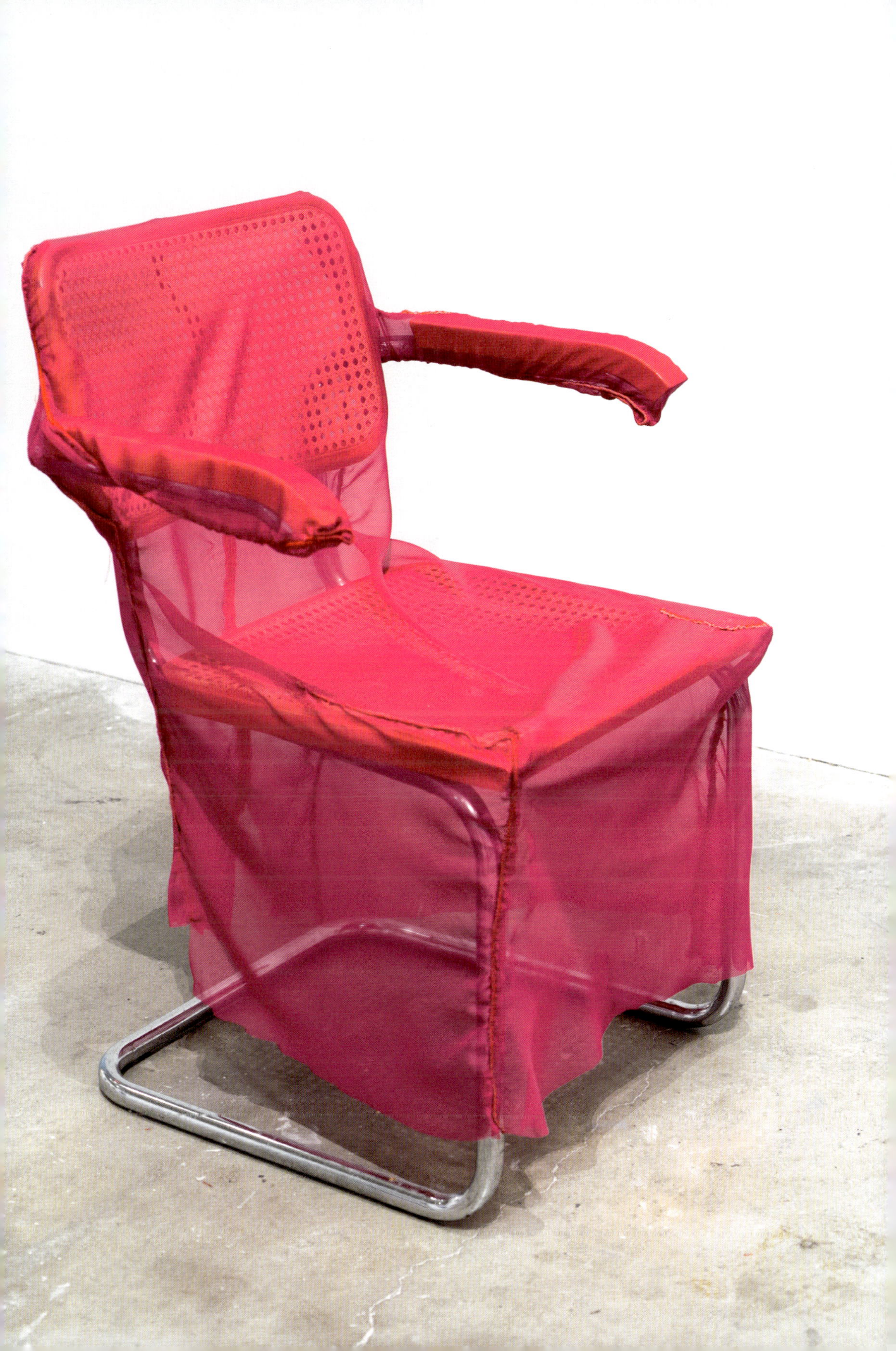

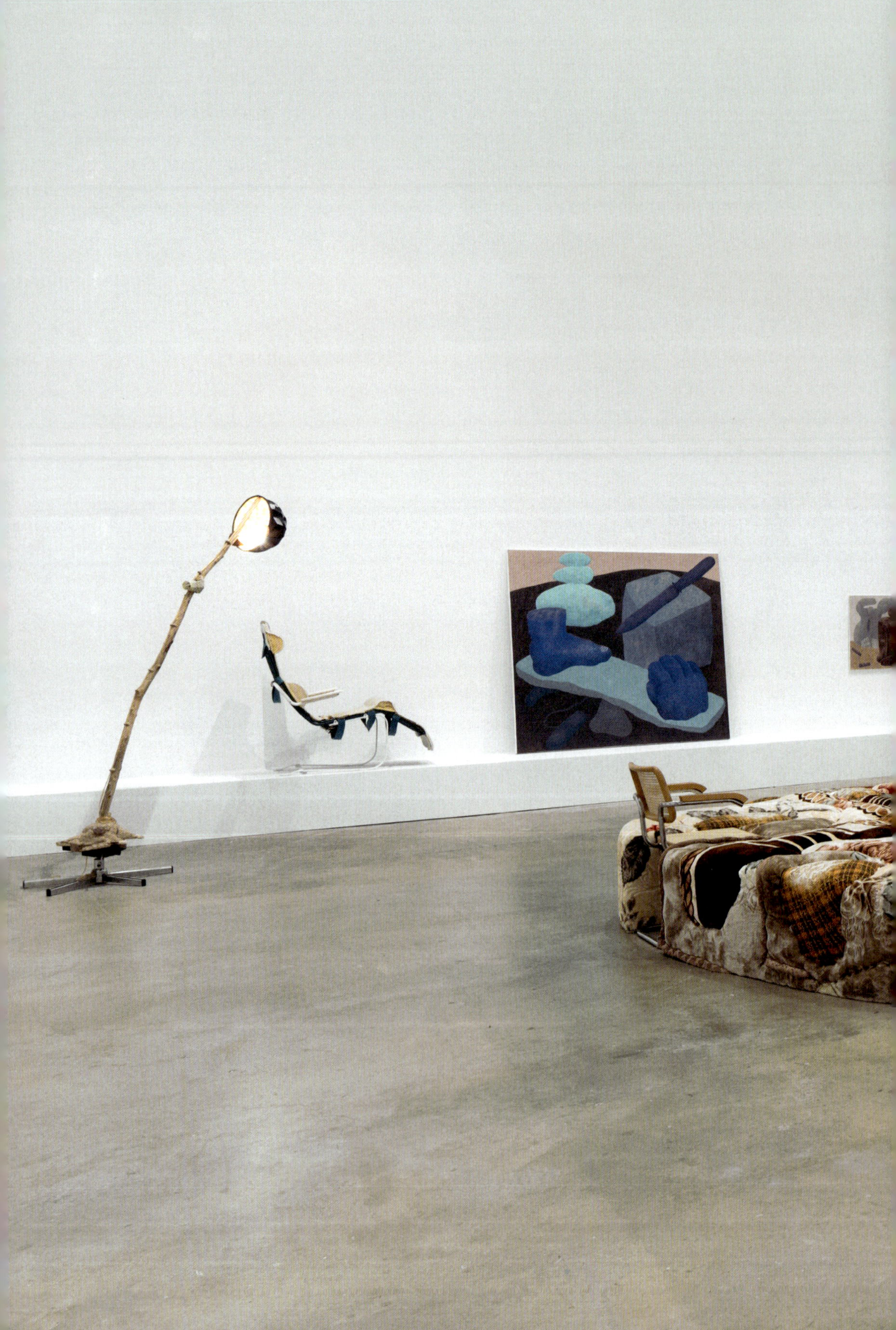

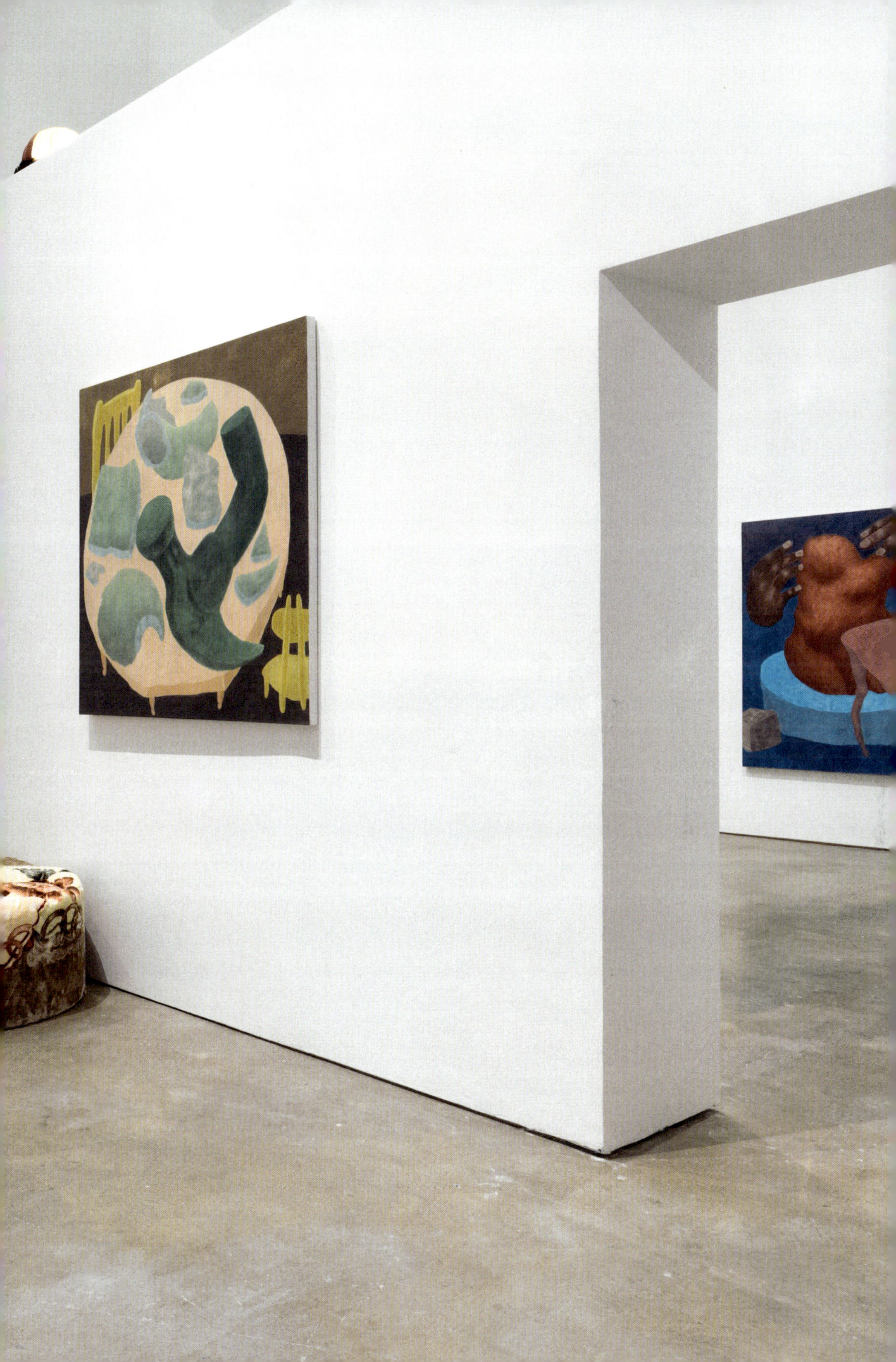

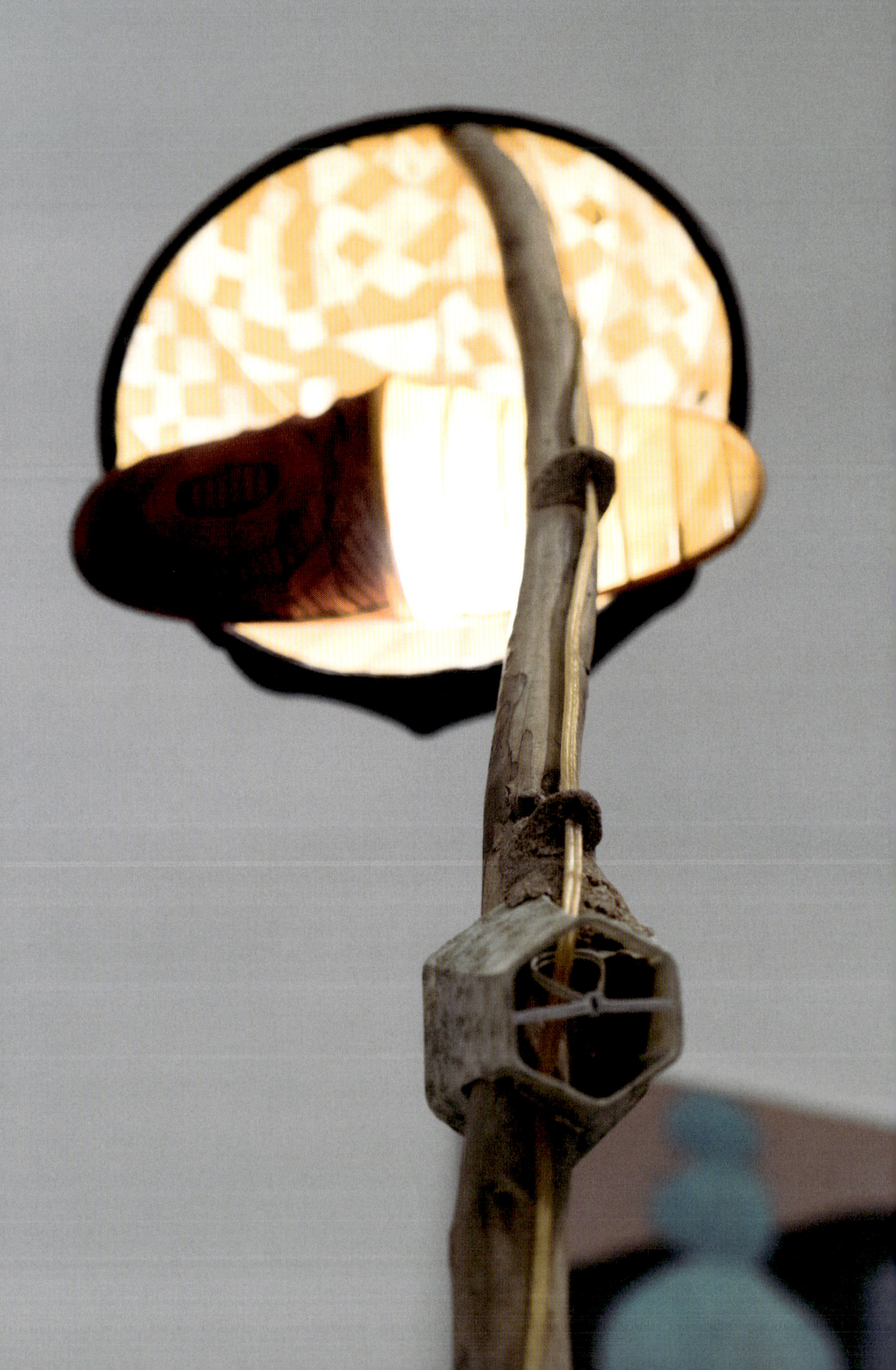

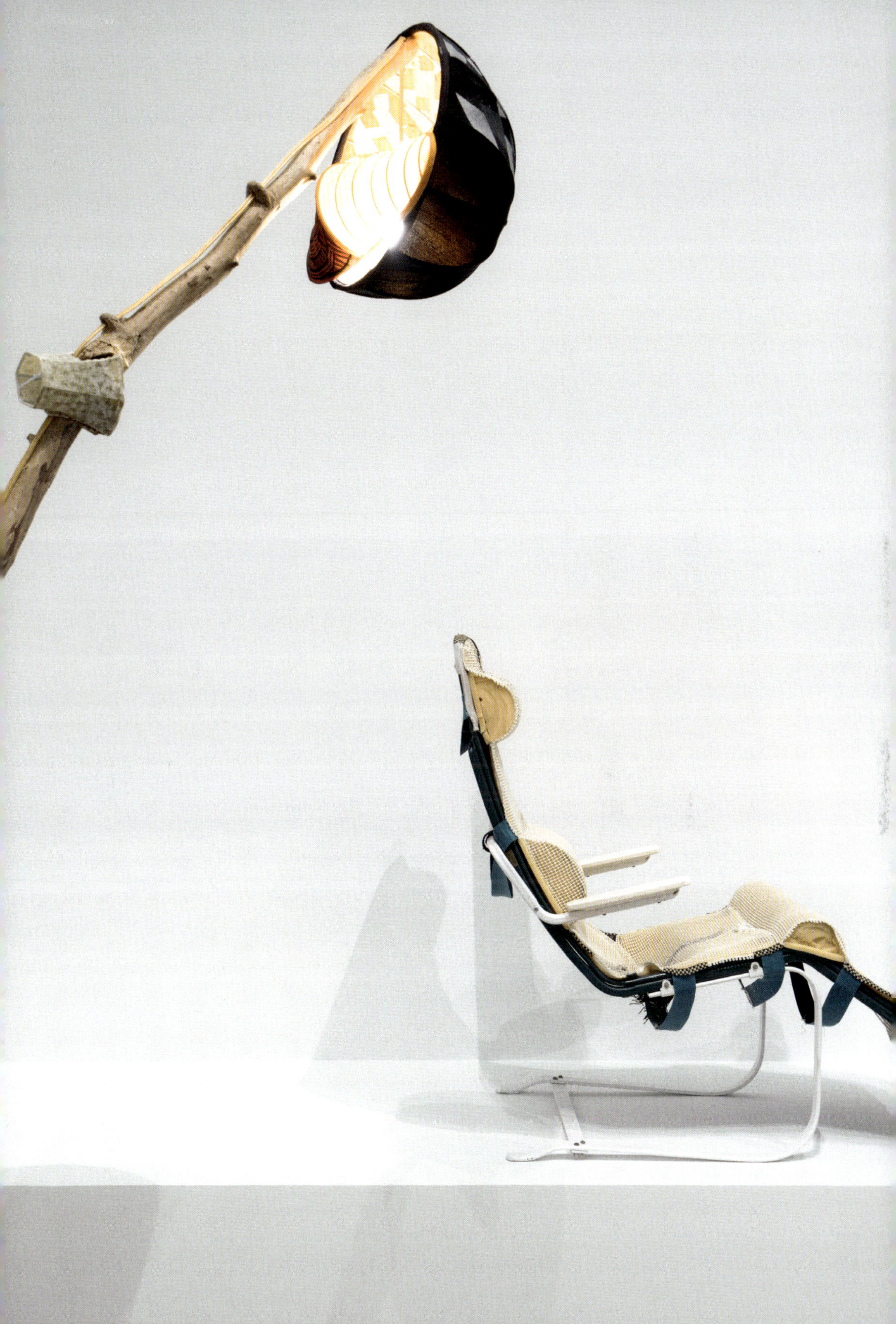

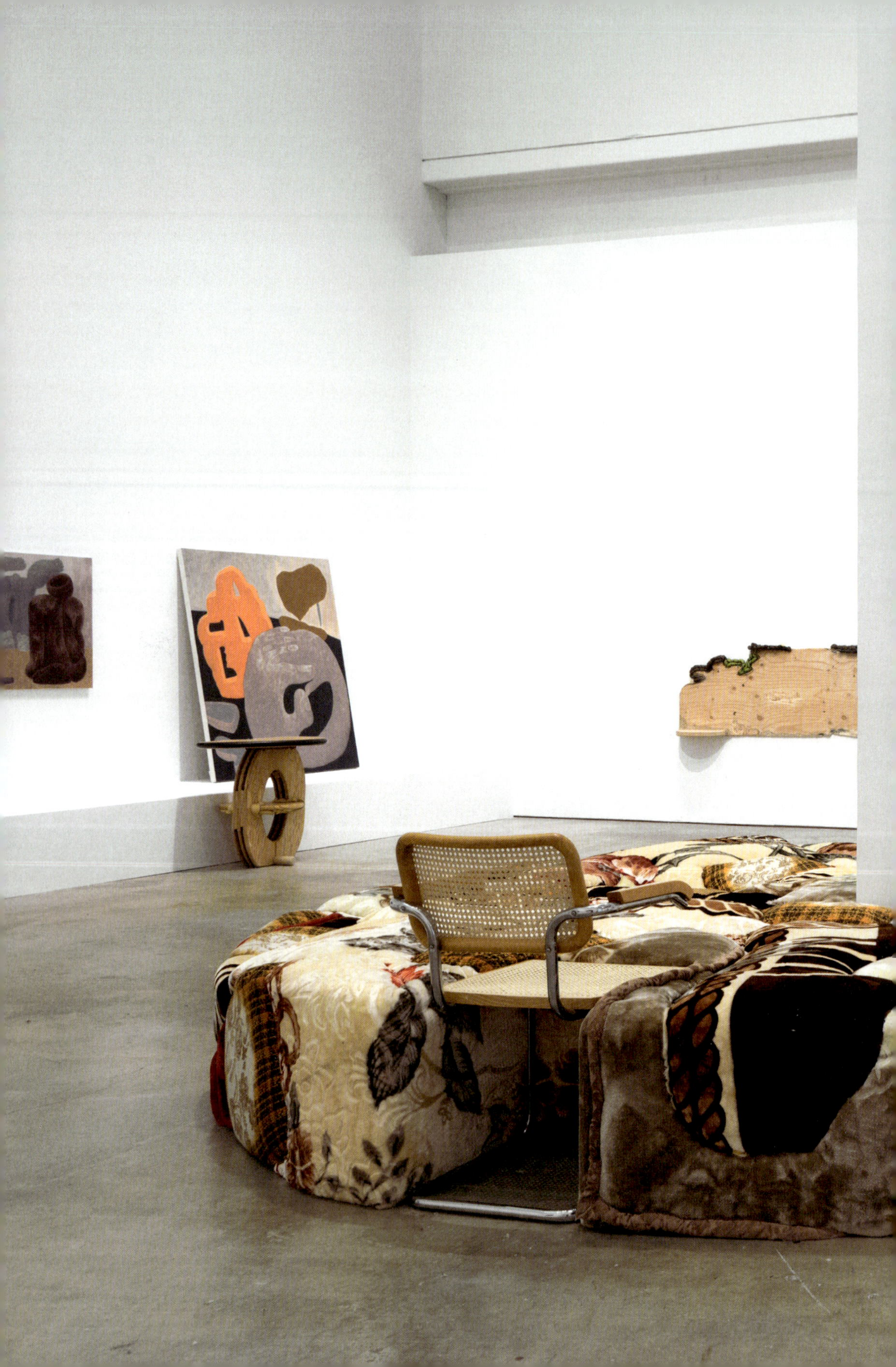

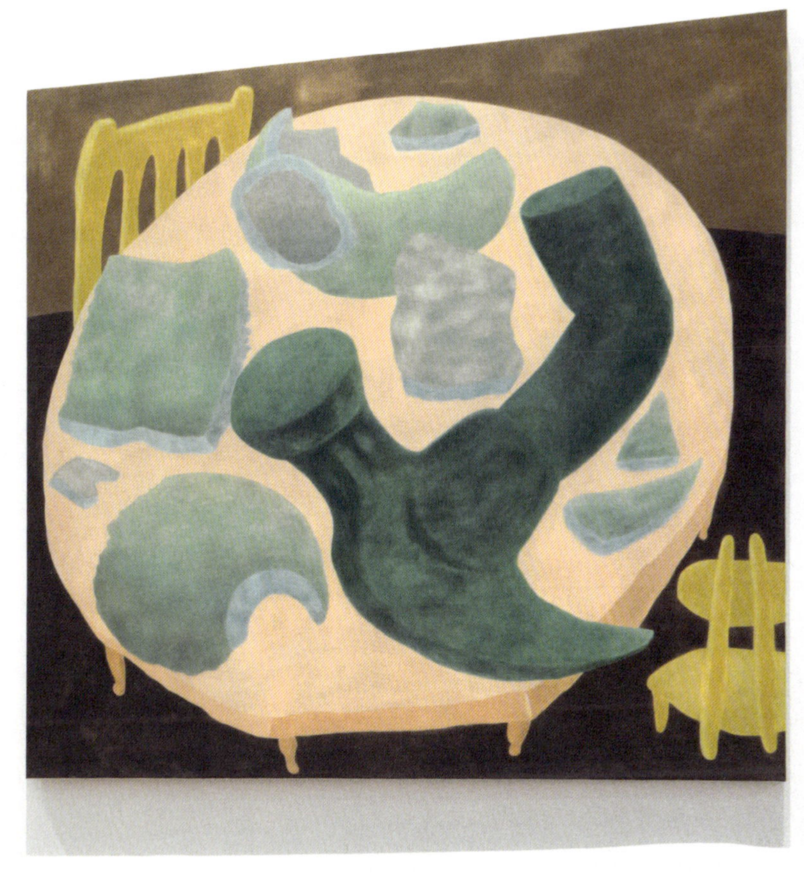
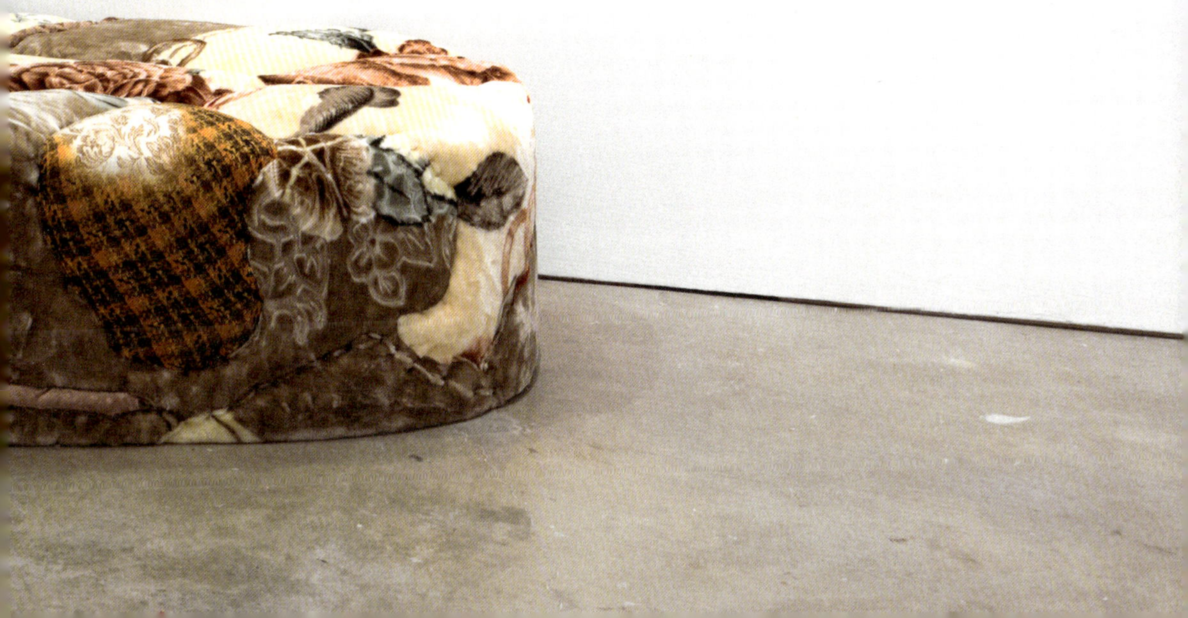

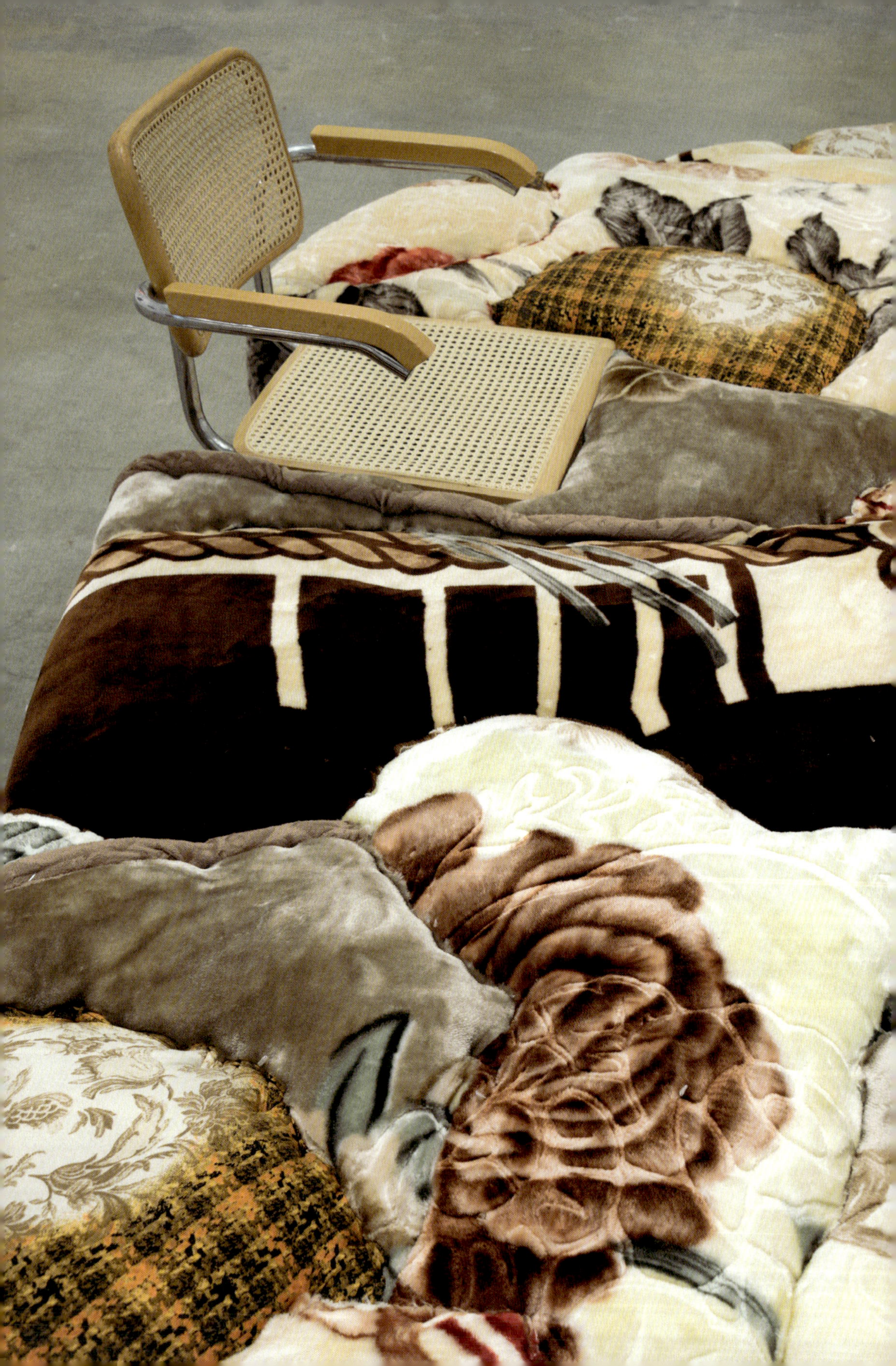

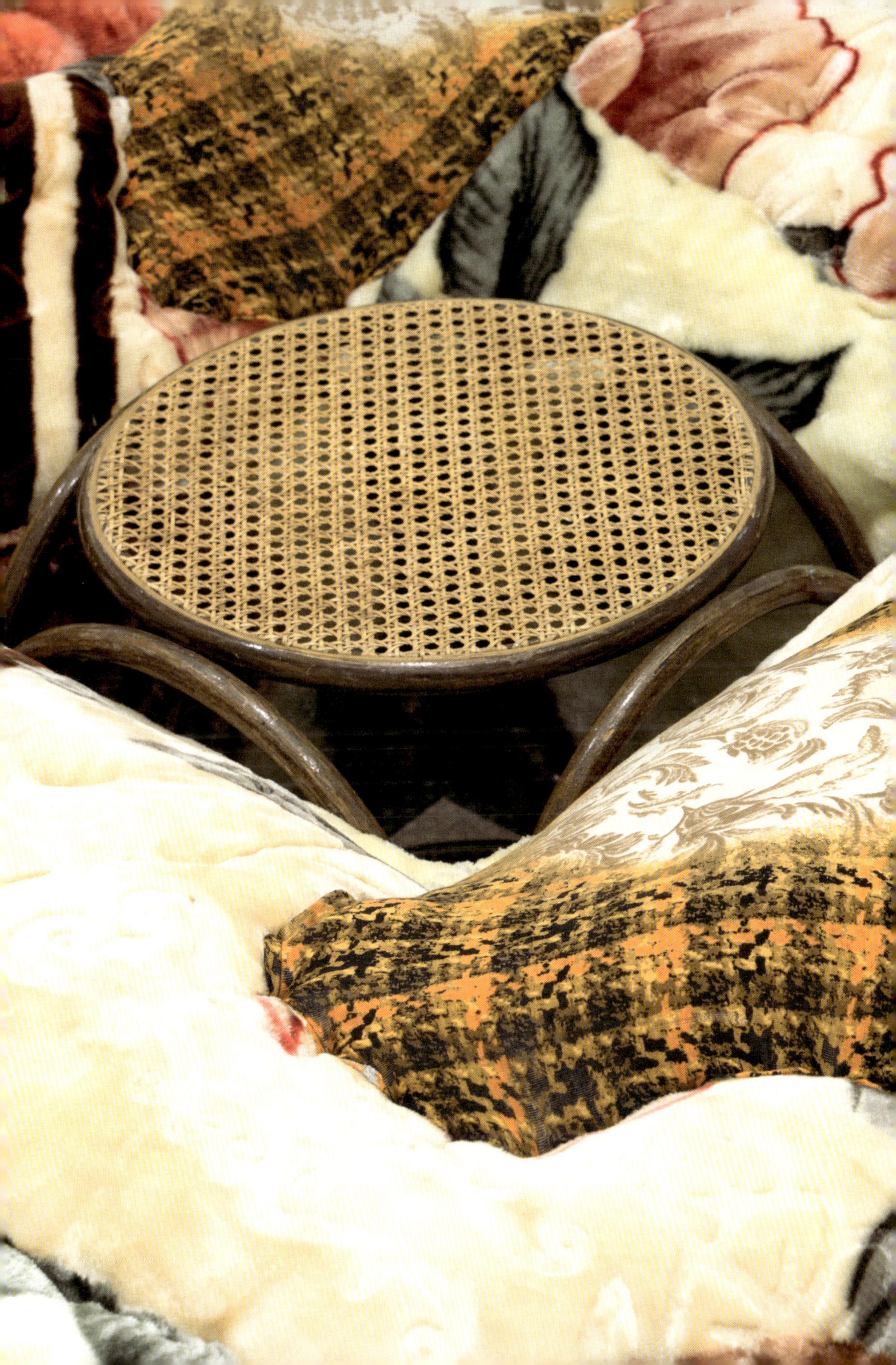

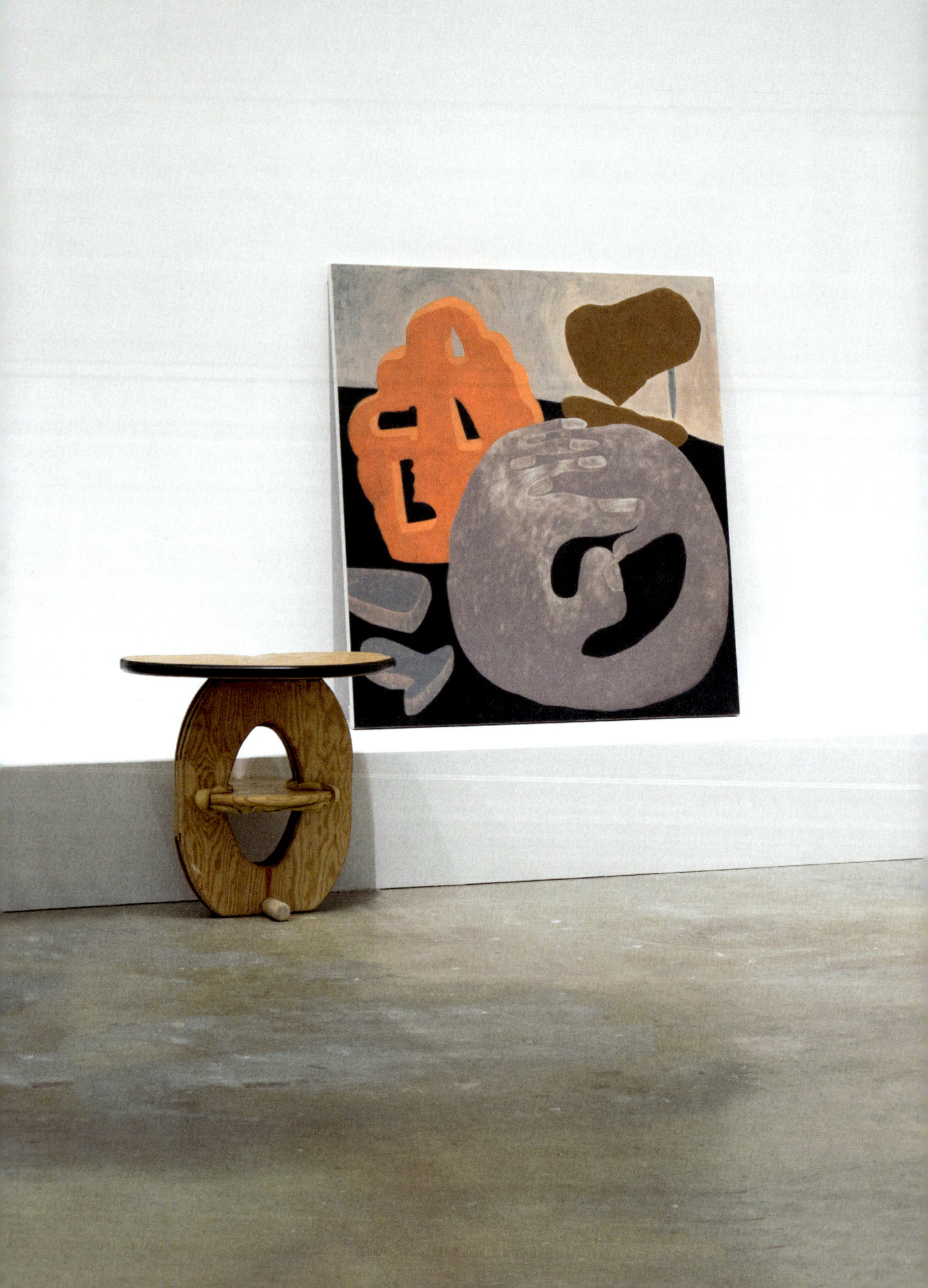

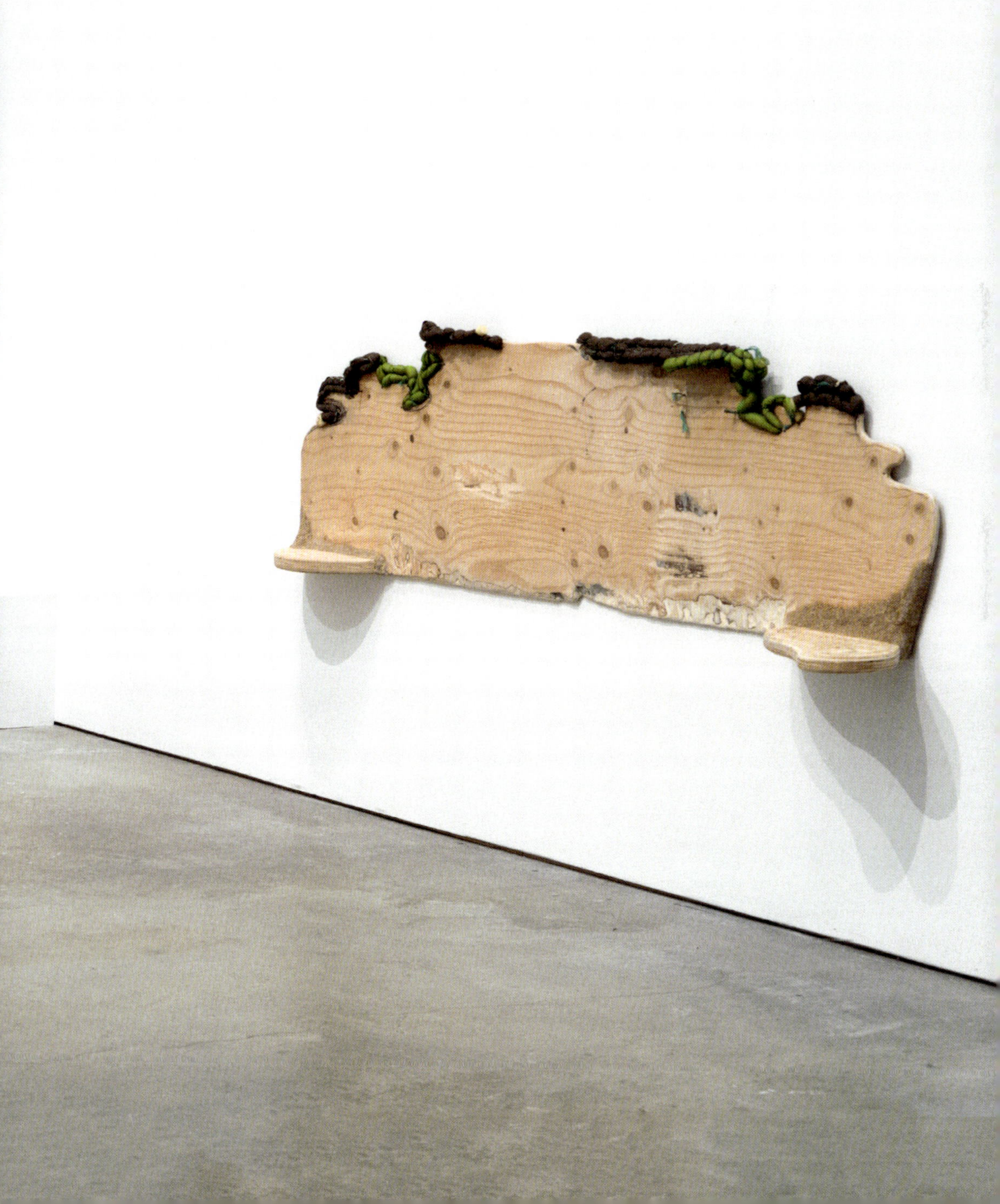

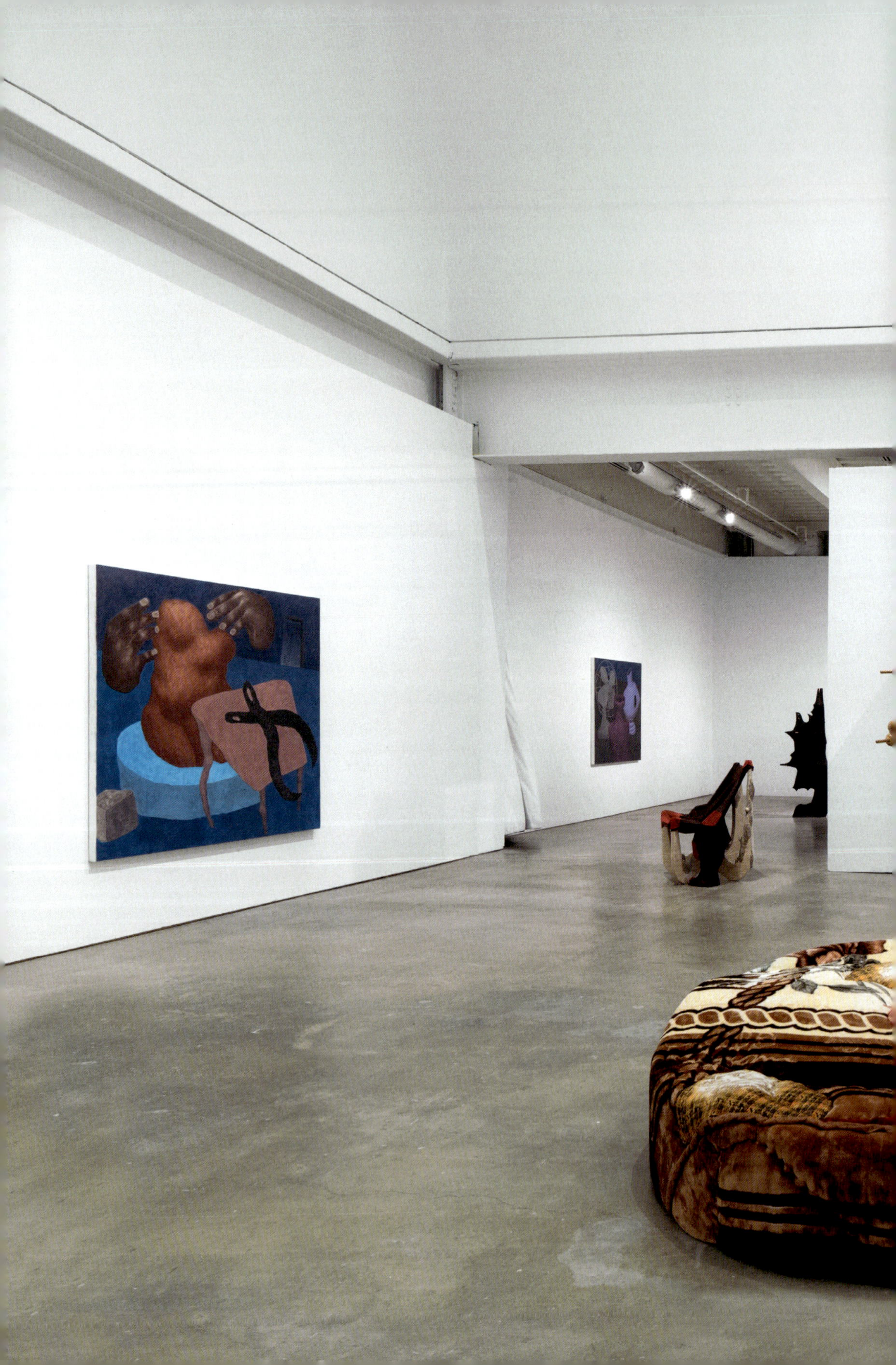

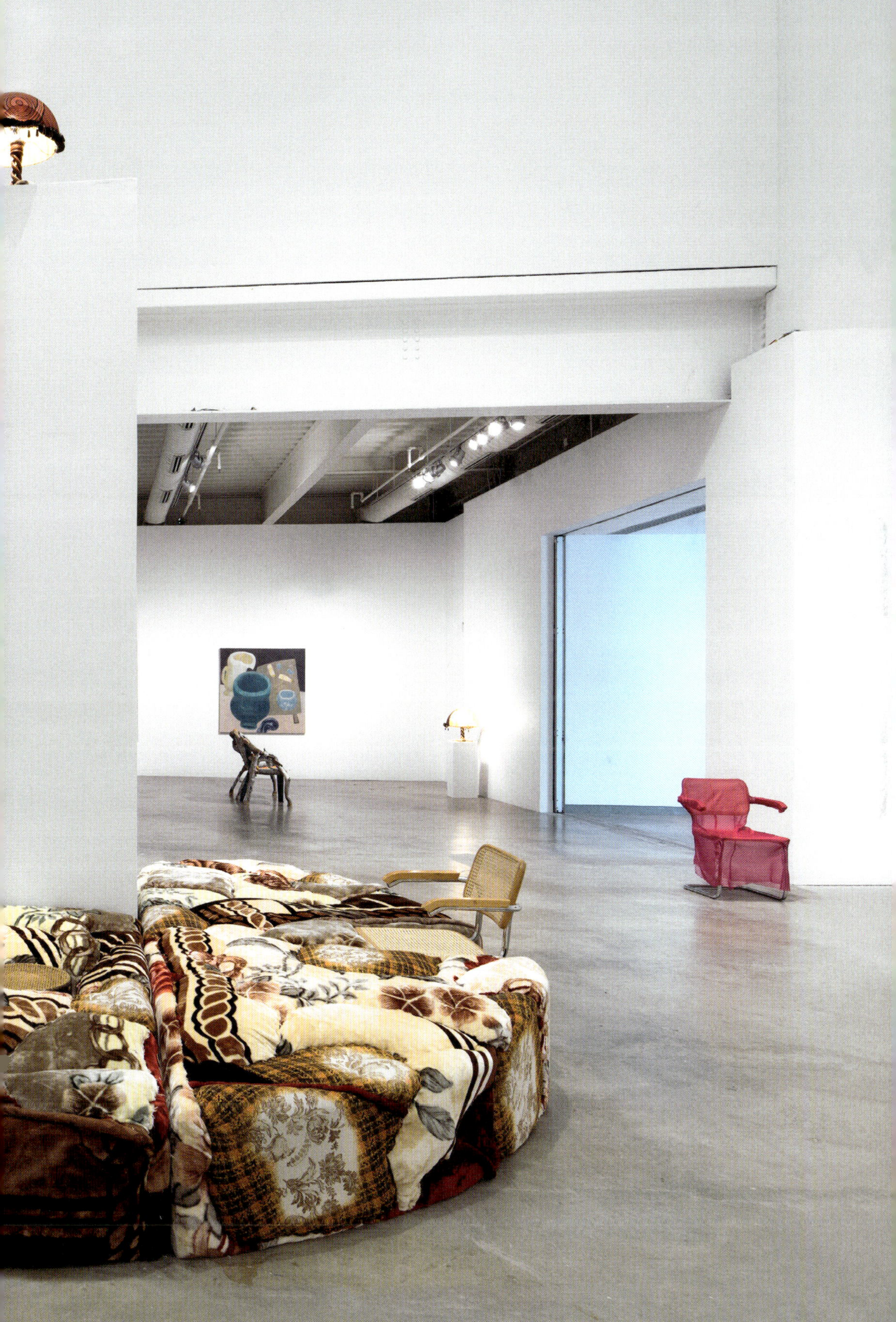

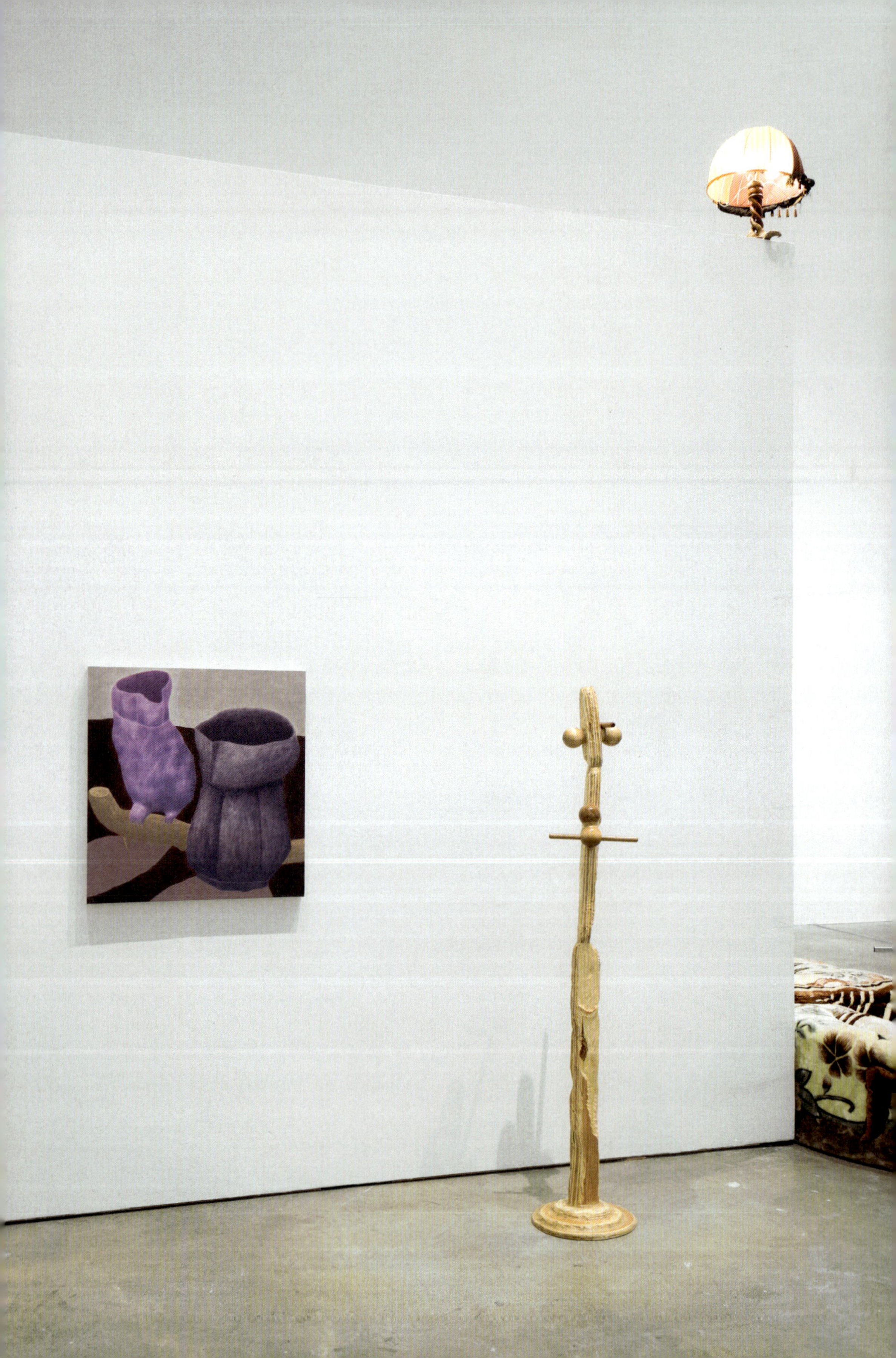

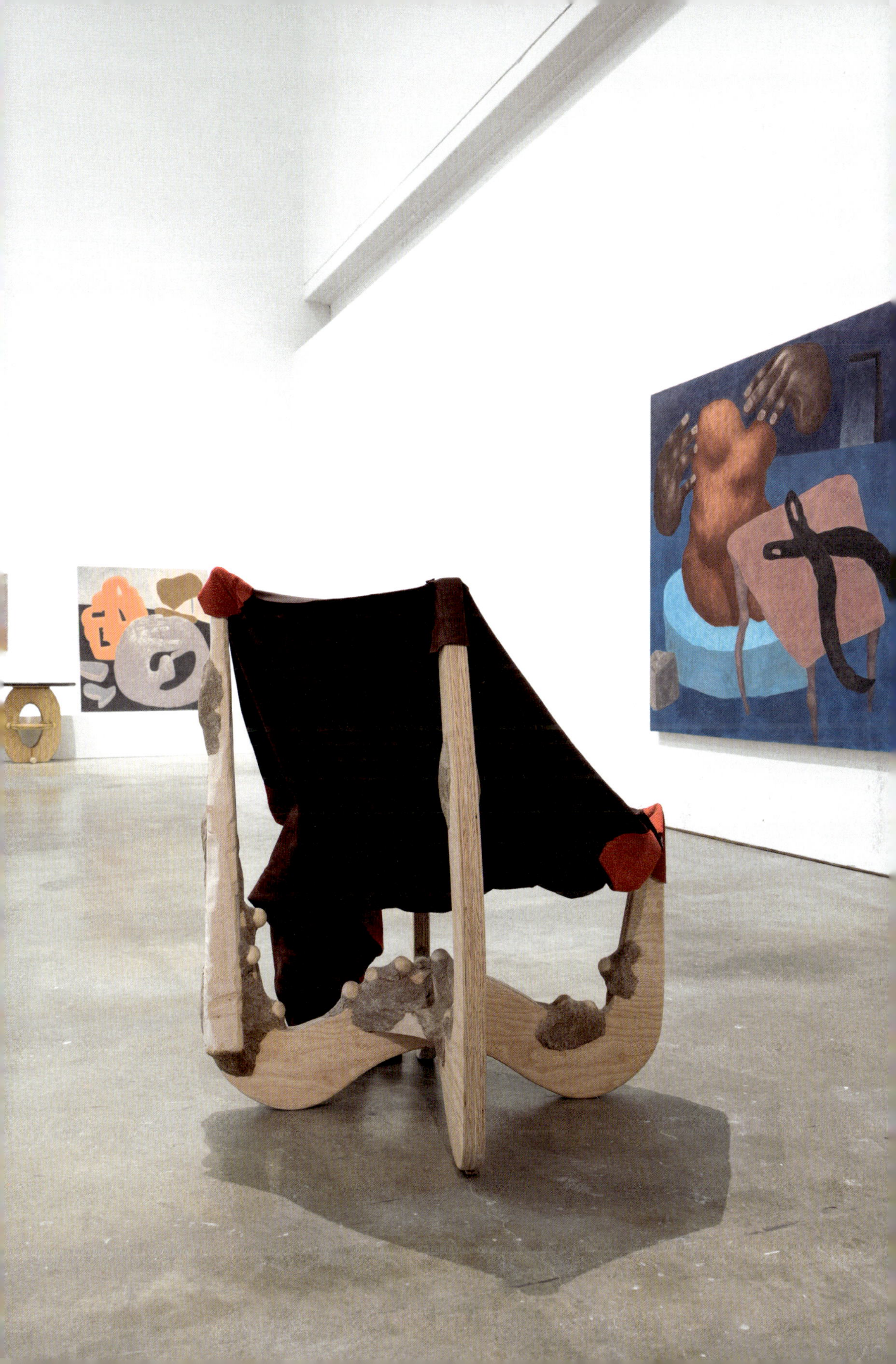

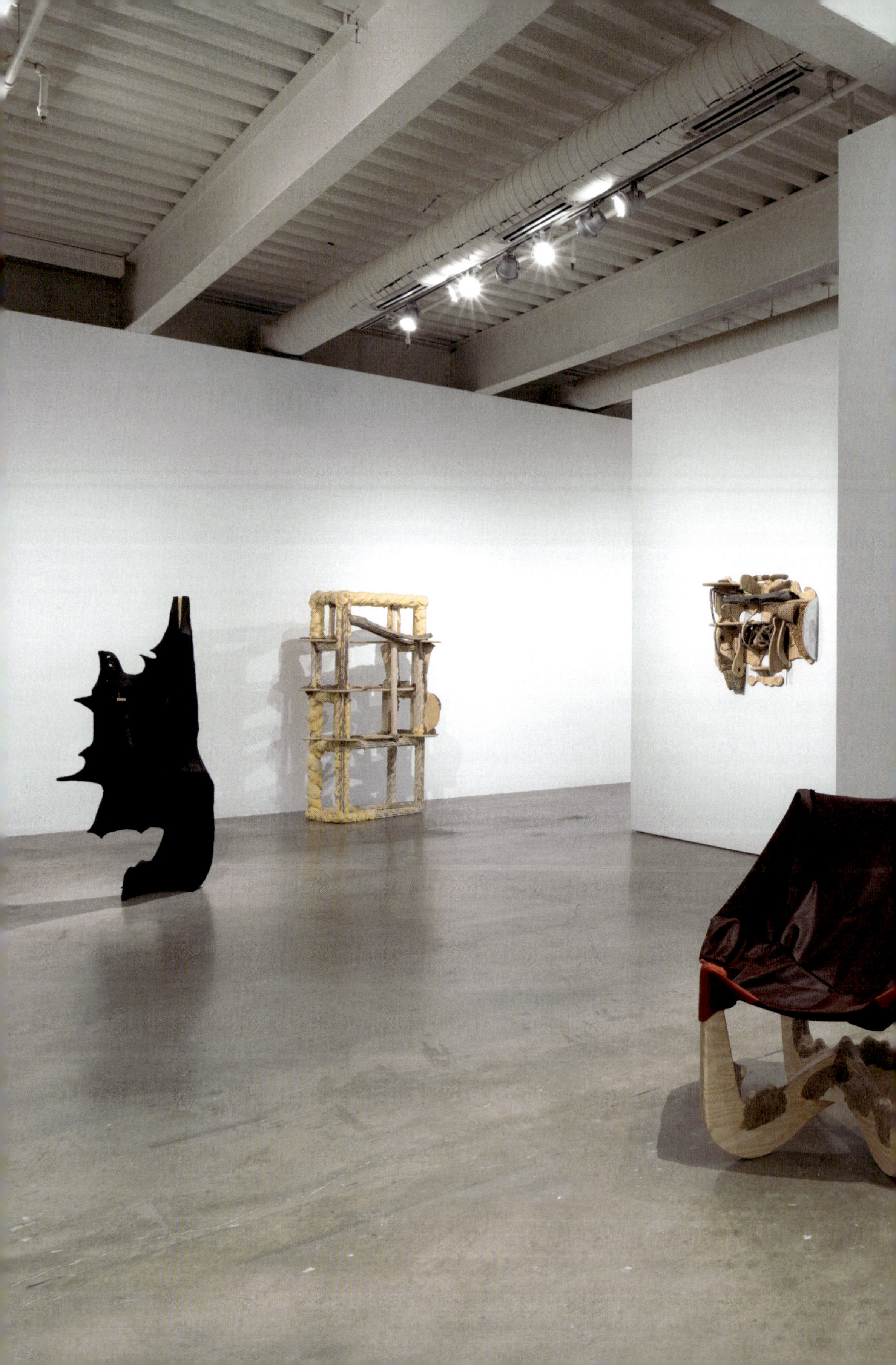

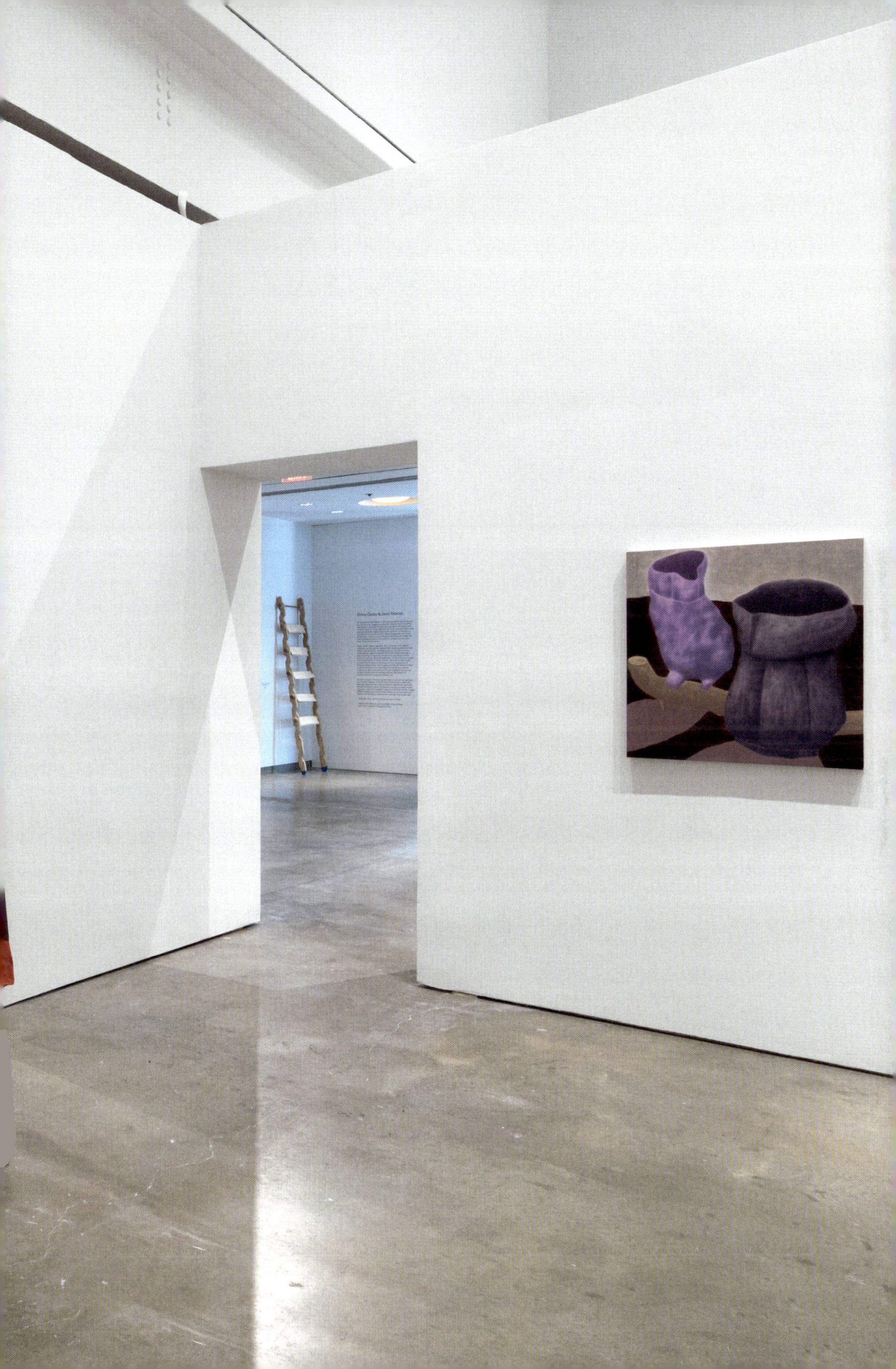
Ginny Casey & Jessi Reaves

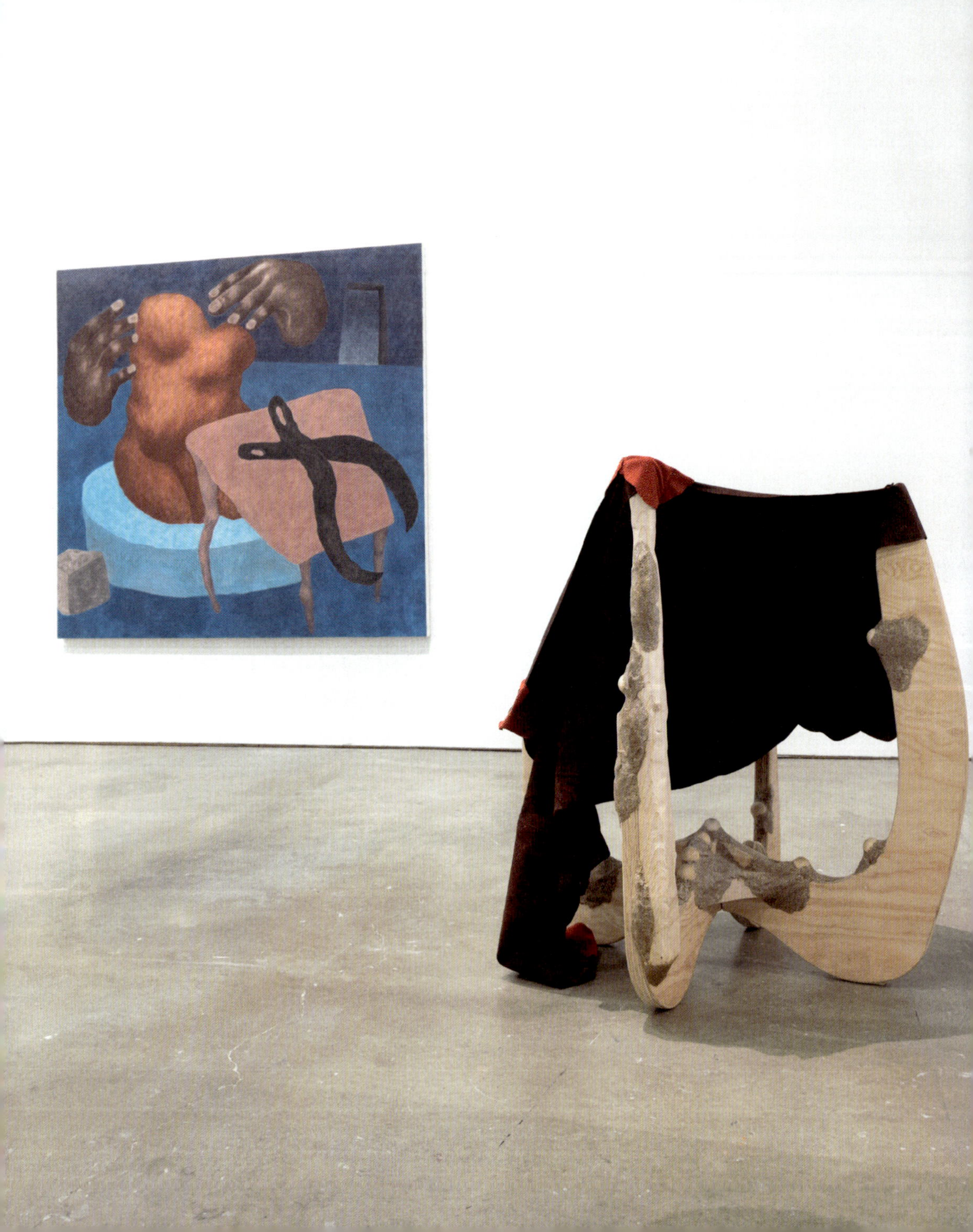

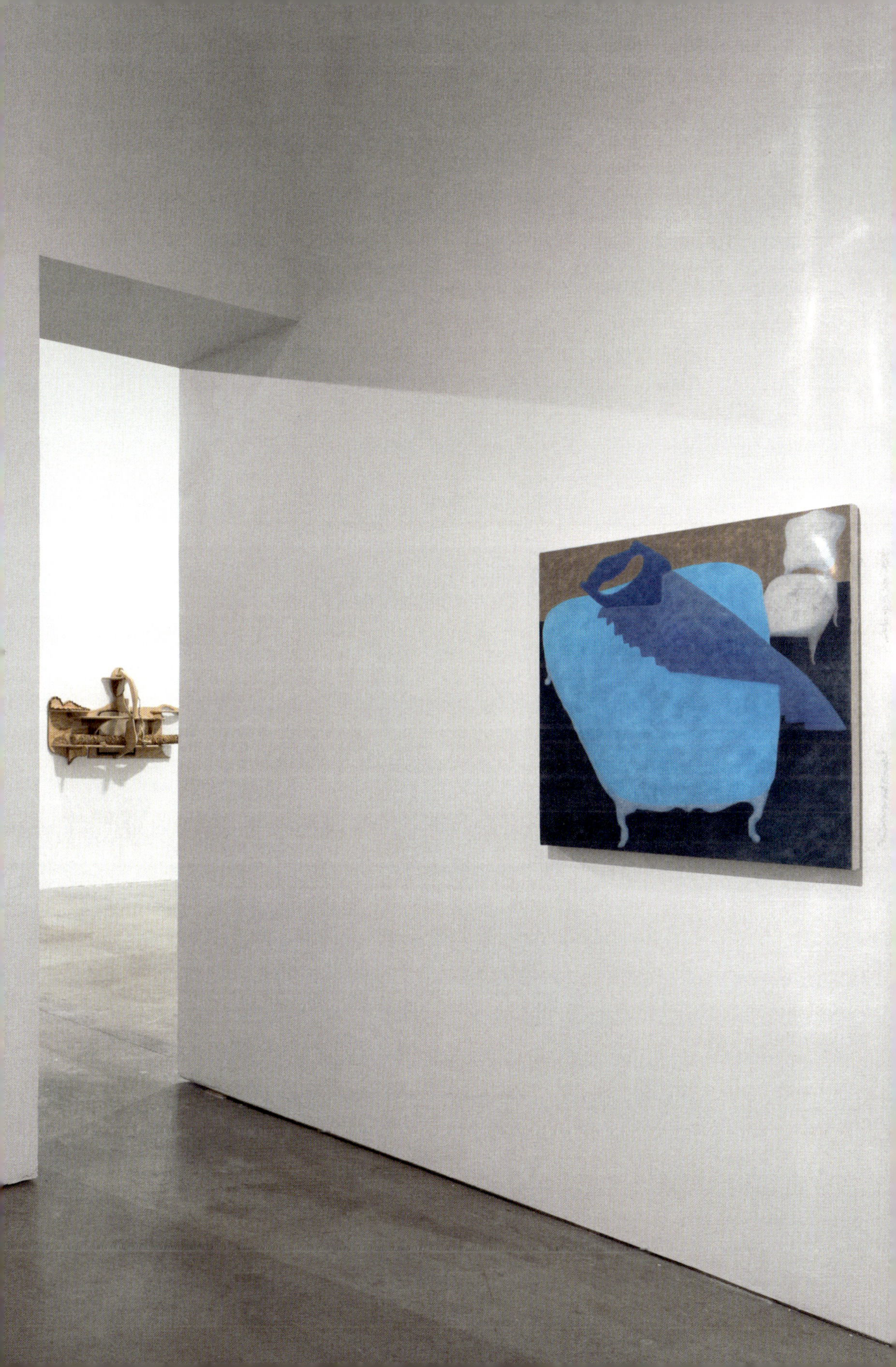

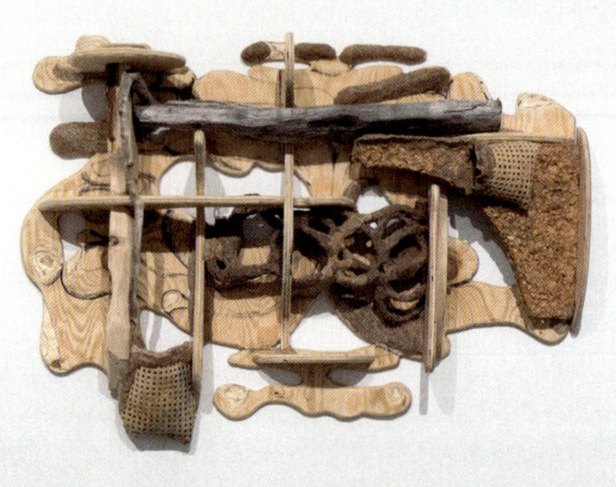

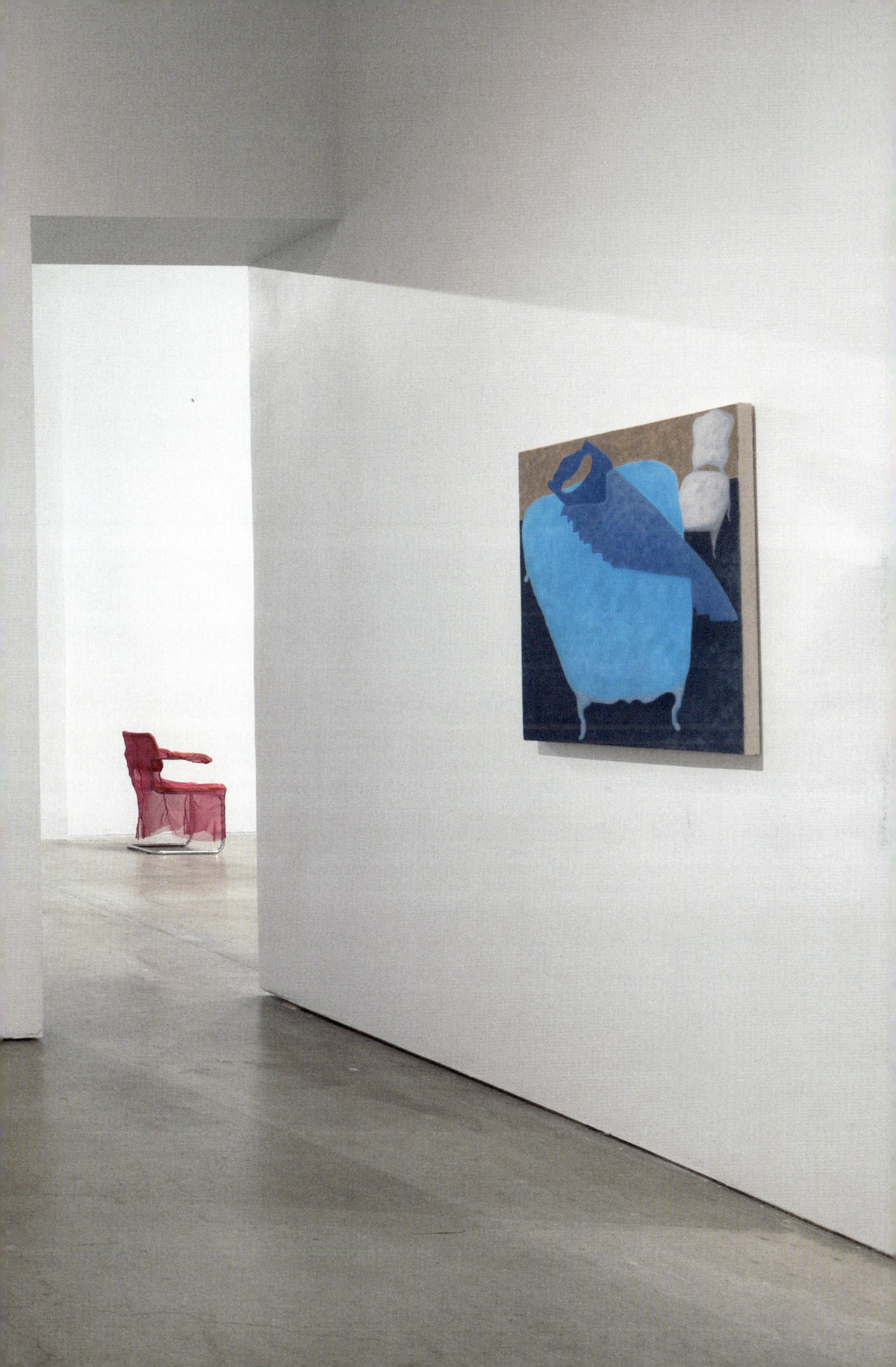

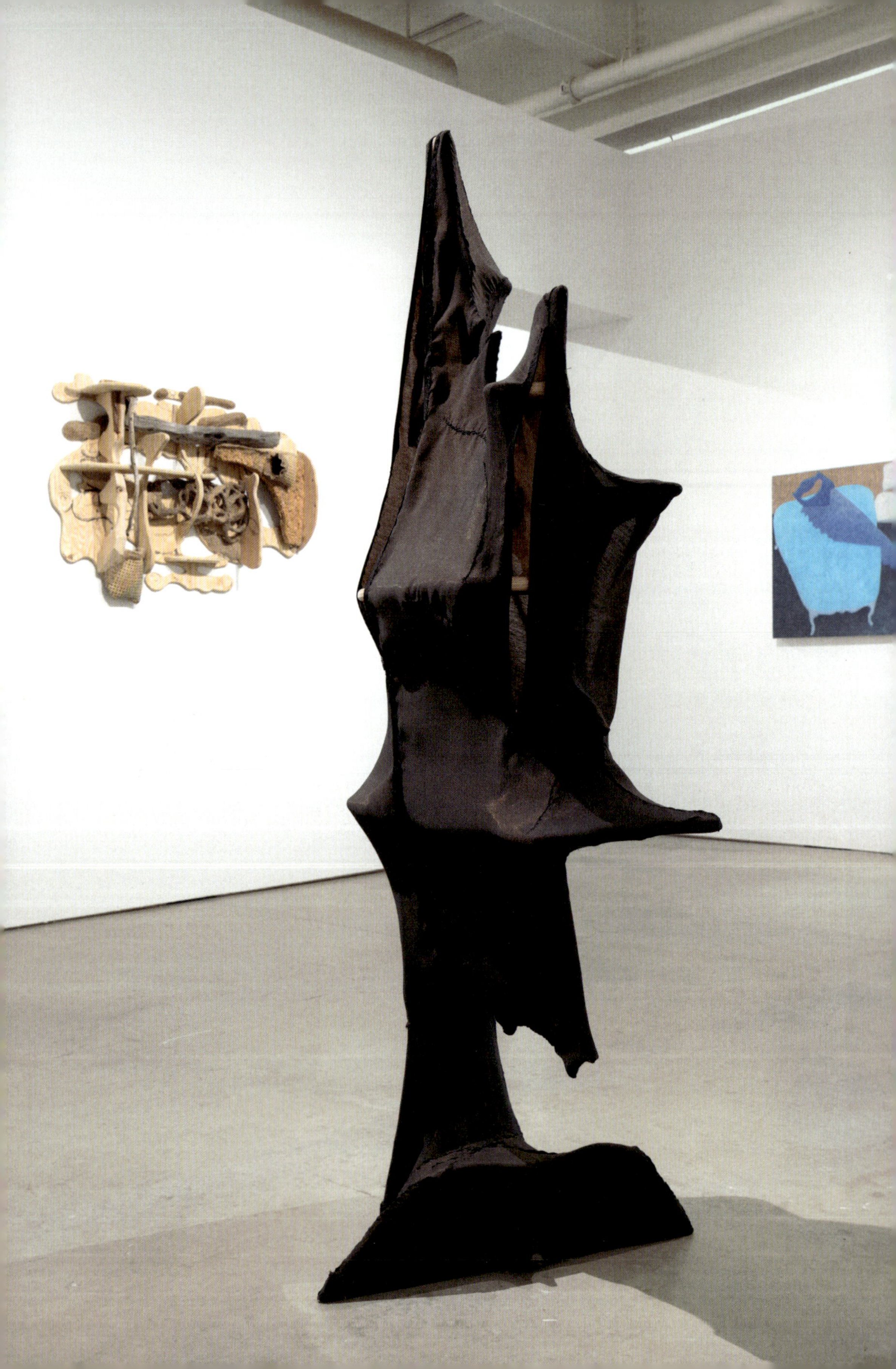

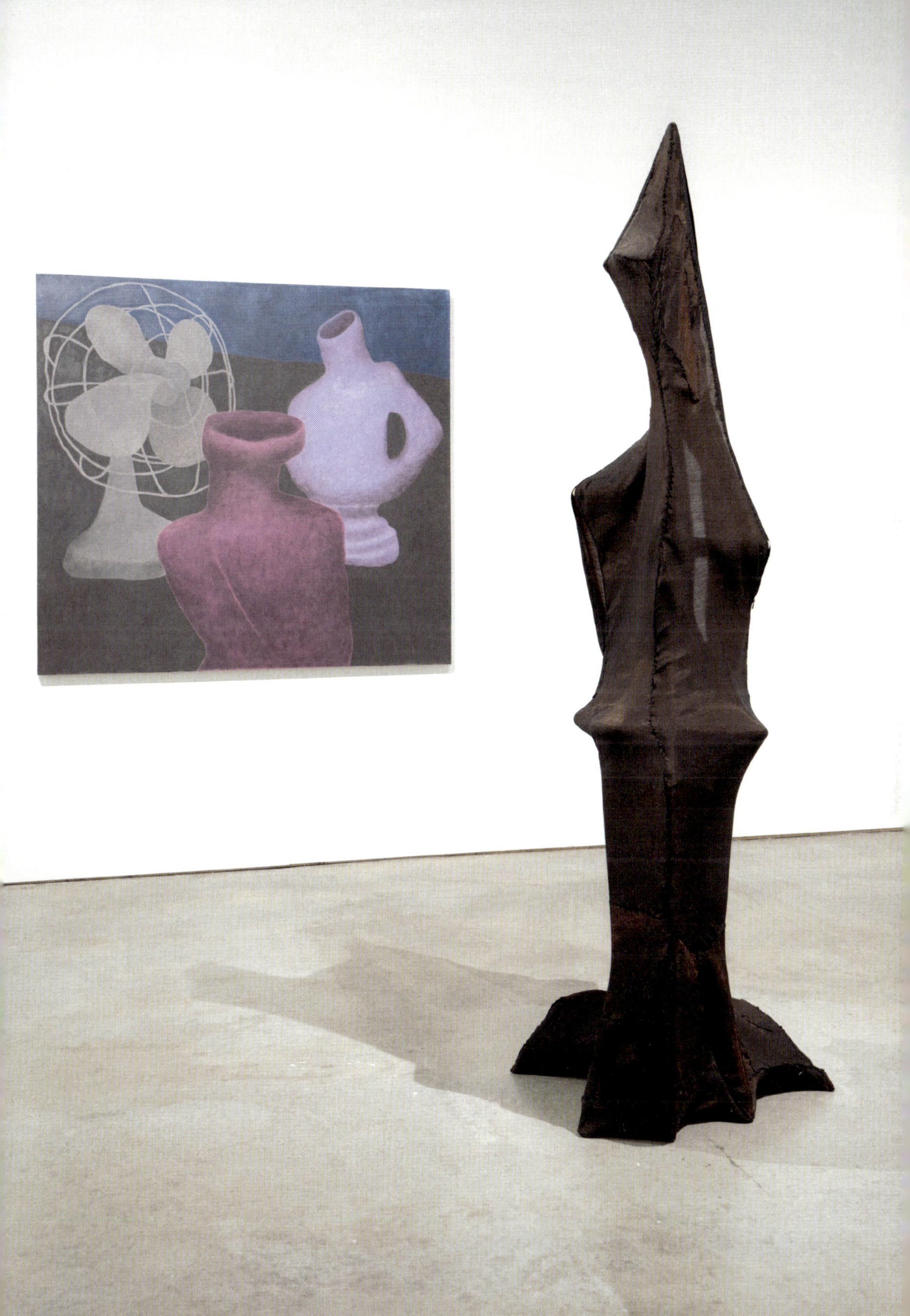

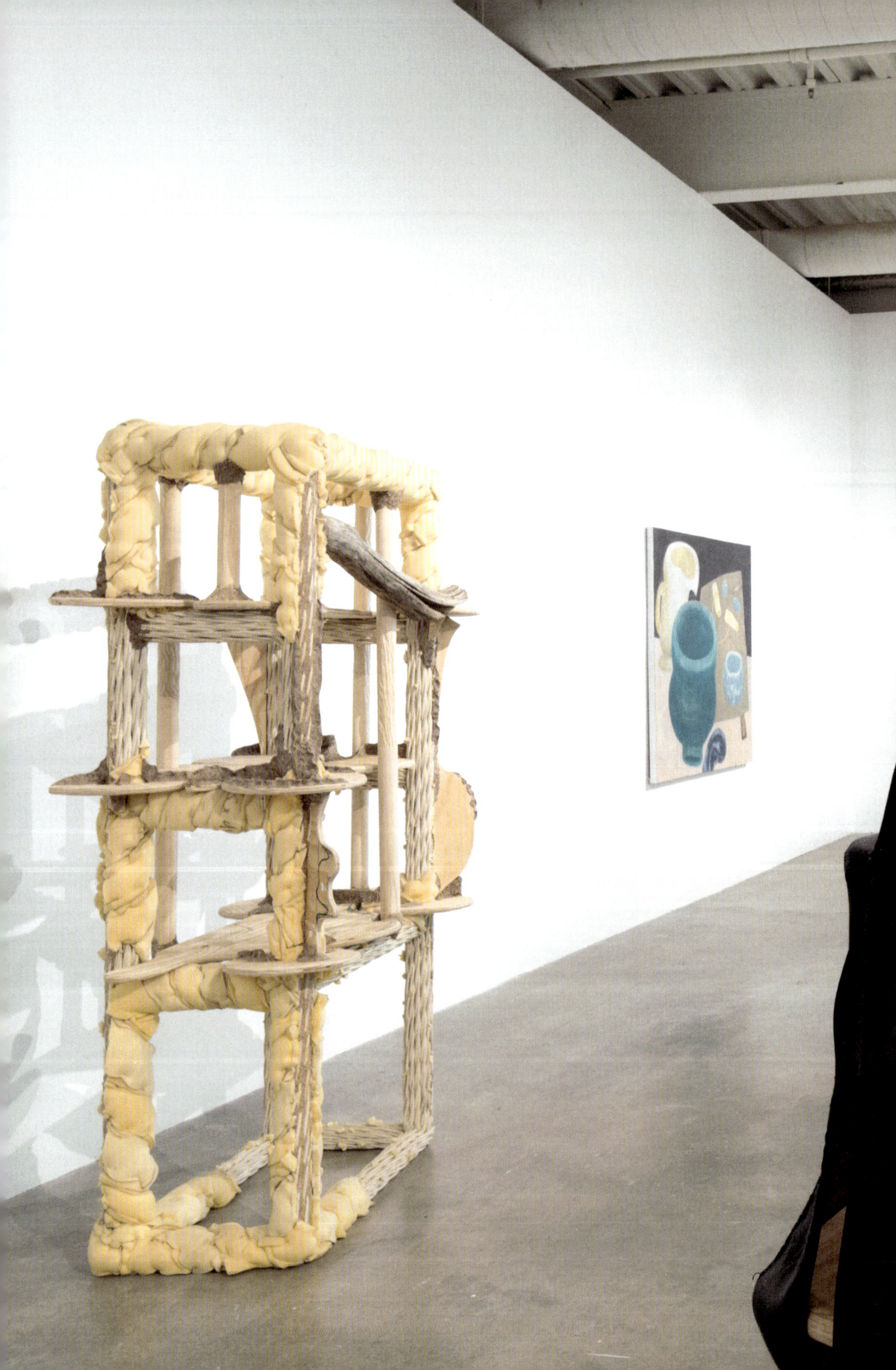

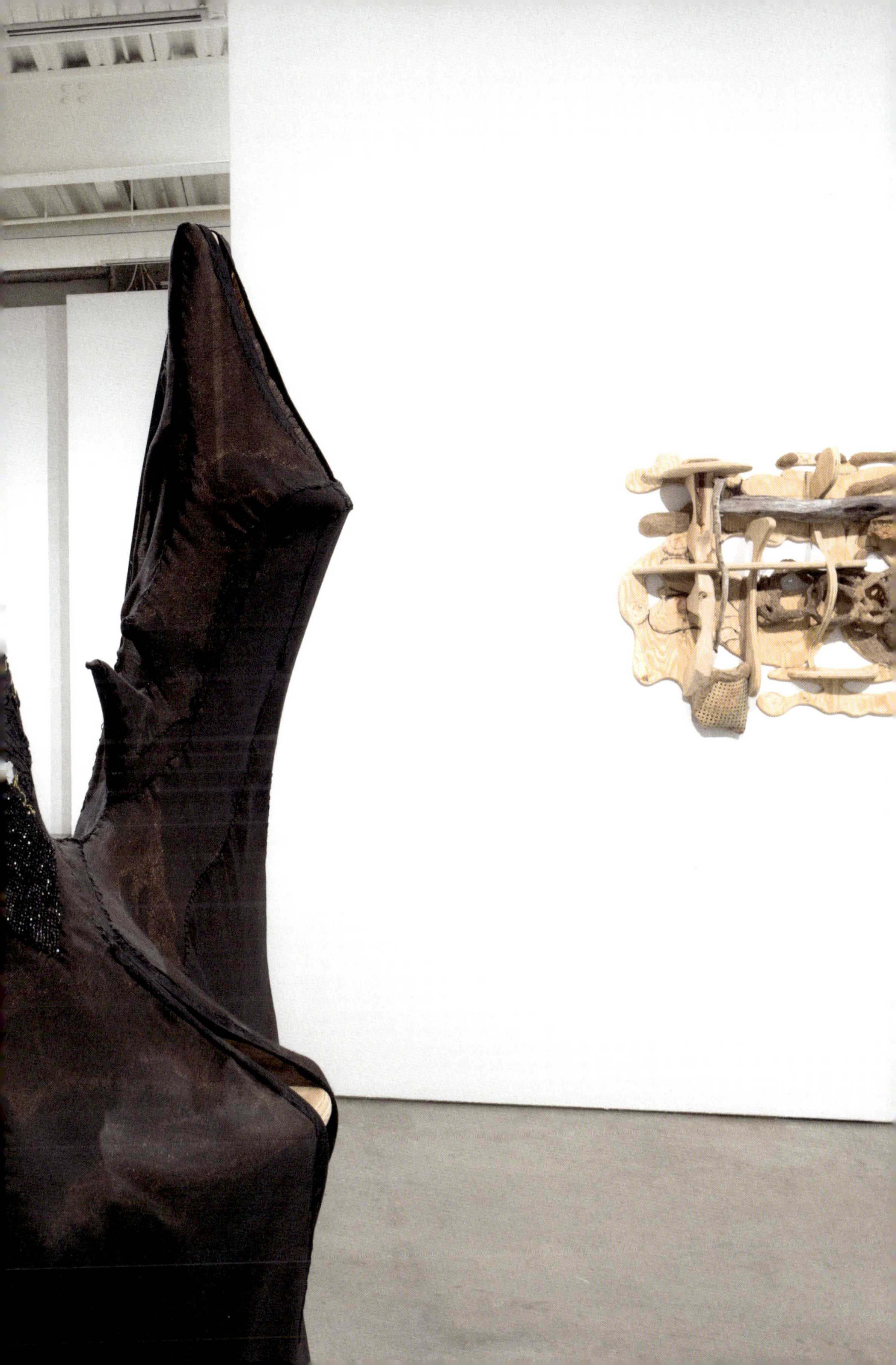

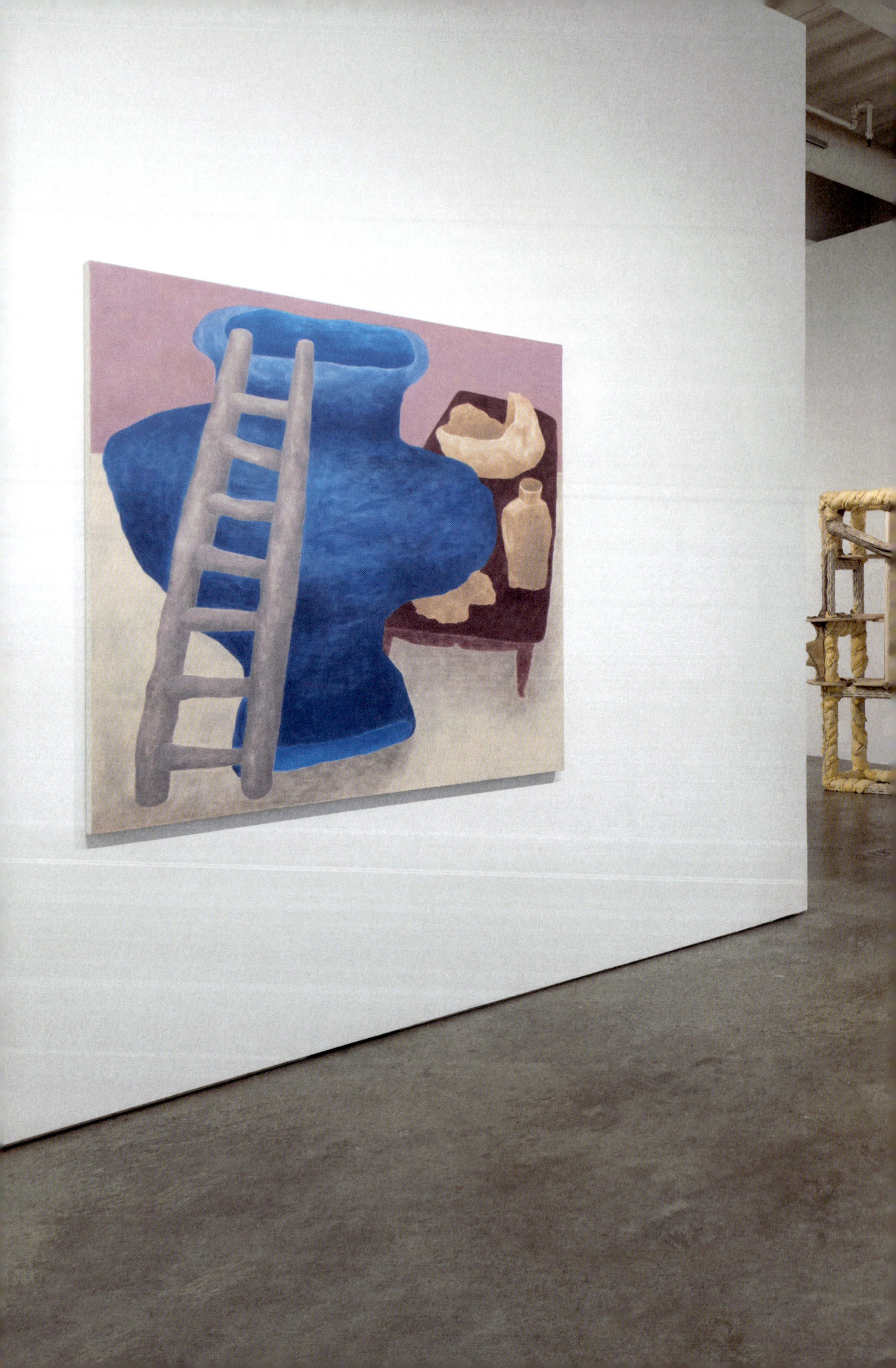

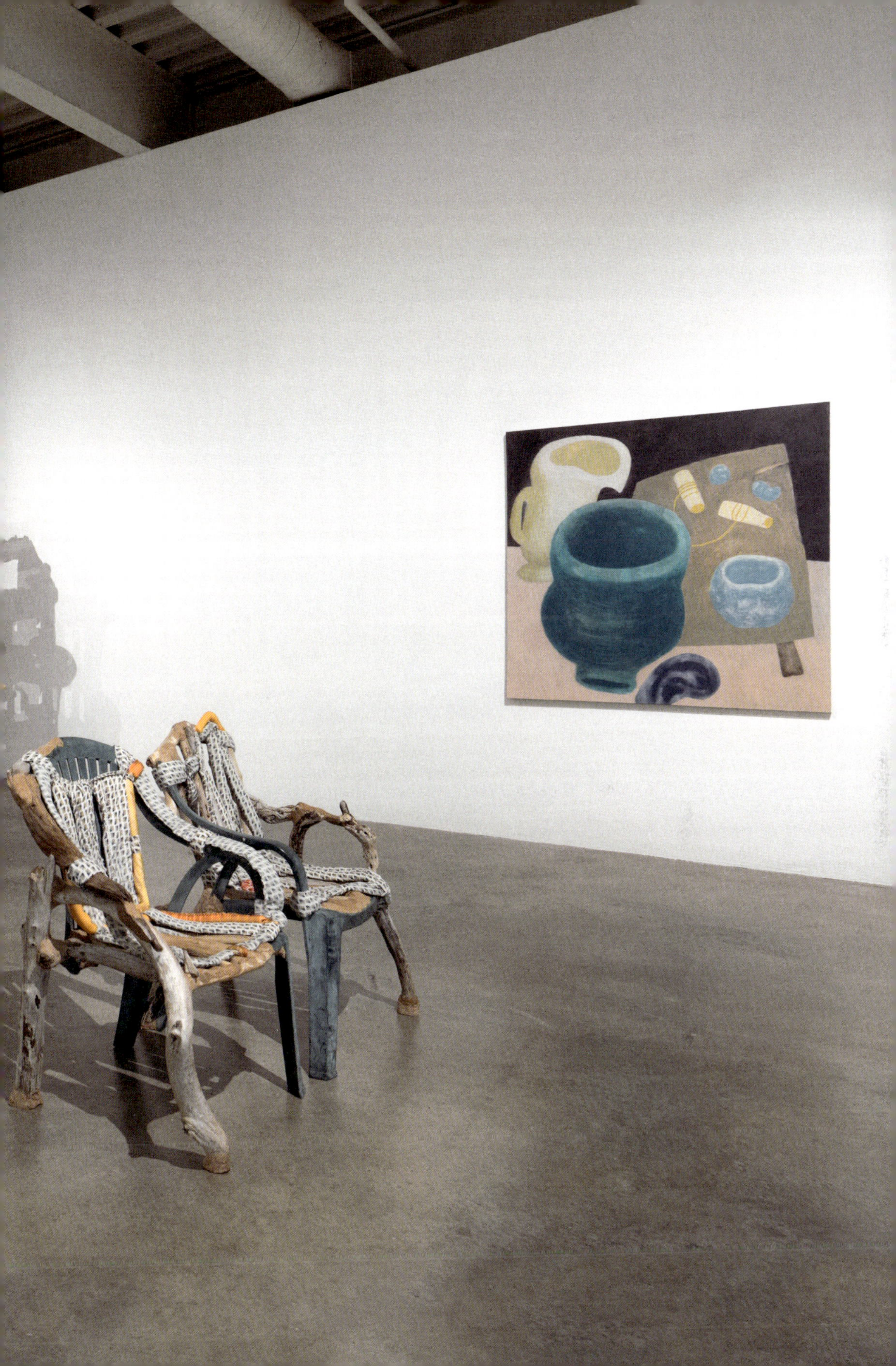

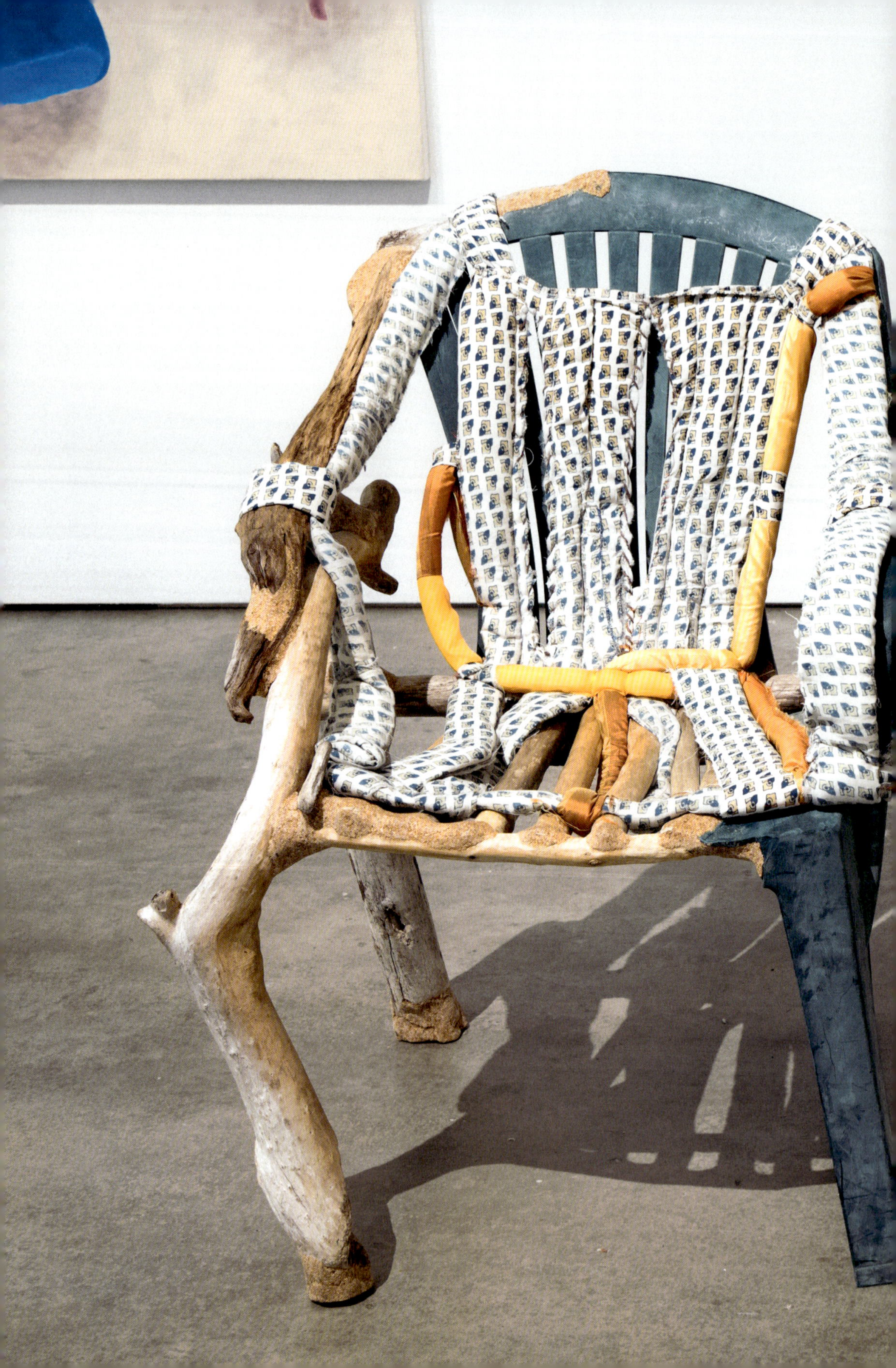

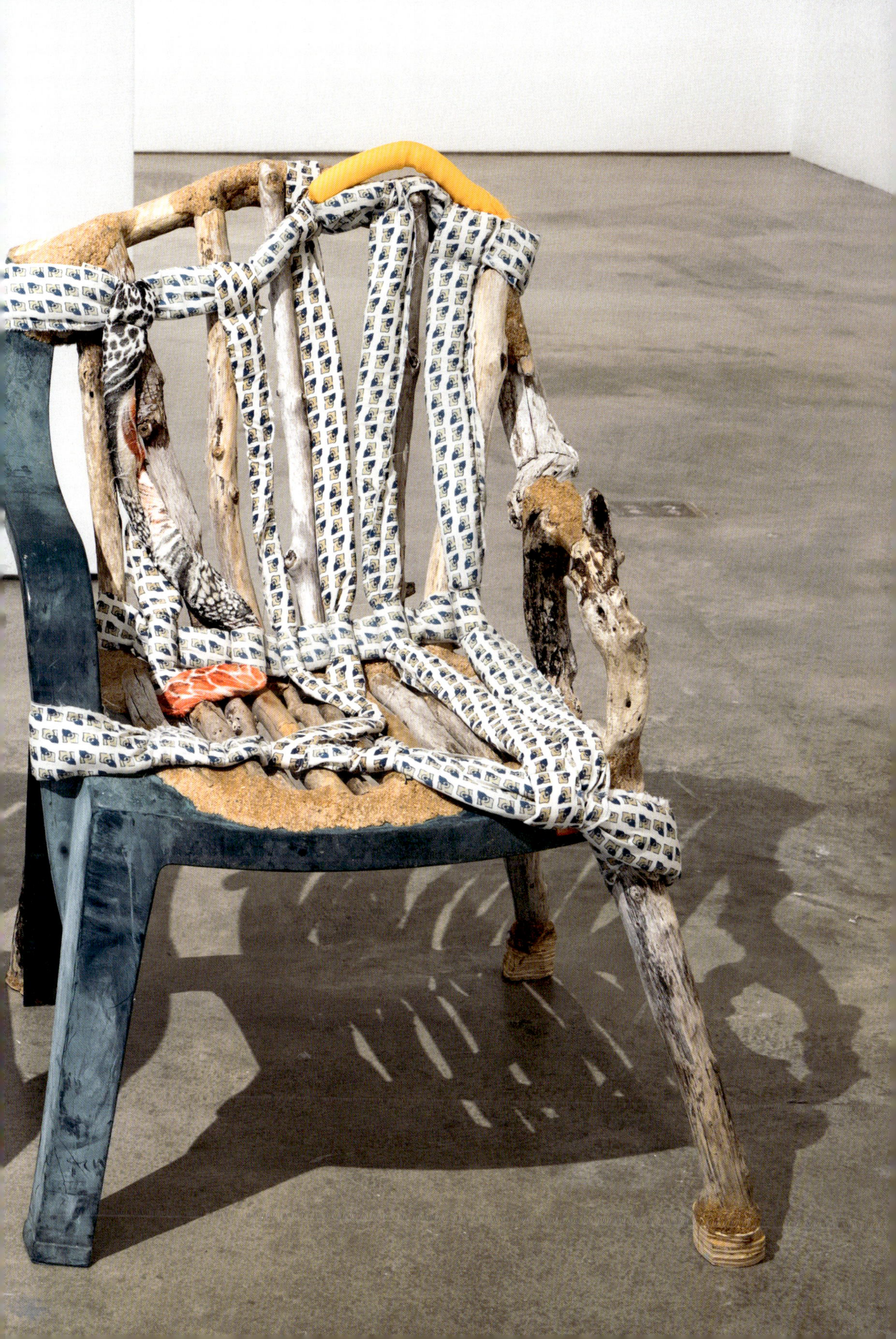

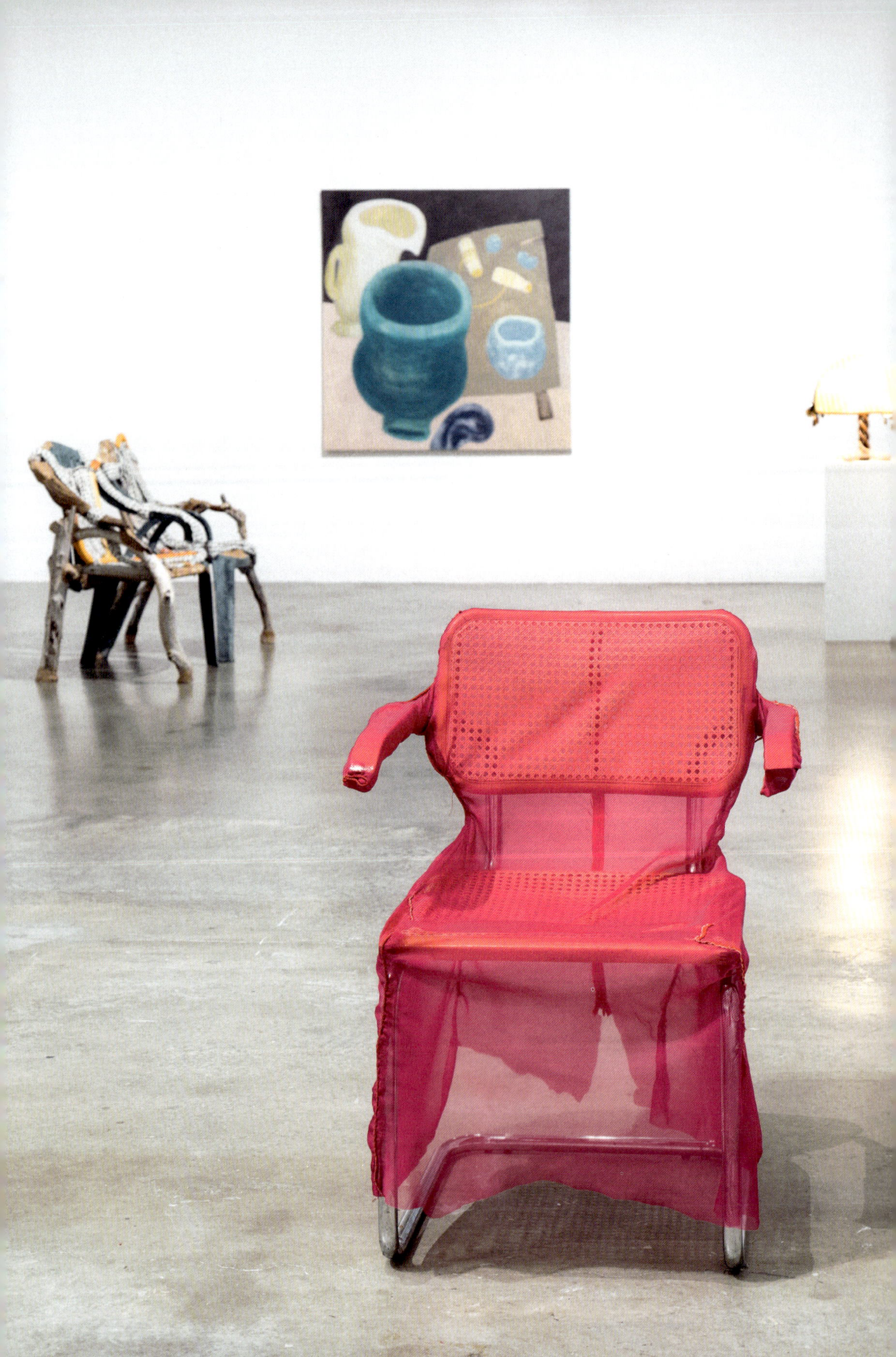

Take a Seat: Ginny Casey and Jessi Reaves

Julia Bryan-Wilson

It is one of the most frequently cited—and disparaged—passages written by an artist in the history of Western modern and contemporary art:

> *What I dream of is an art of balance, of purity and serenity, devoid of troubling or depressing subject matter, an art that could be for every mental worker, for the businessman as well as the man of letters, for example, a soothing, calming influence on the mind, something like a good armchair which provides relaxation from fatigue.*[1]

Published by Henri Matisse in 1908 in his "Notes of a Painter," the comparison between an ameliorative art and a comfortable armchair has long been taken as proof of Matisse's regressive, non-threatening tendencies, his predilection towards simple decoration aimed at cushioning the bourgeoisie rather than the shock, rupture, and pictorial violence offered by some of his rivals who attempted to transgress conventional values in both form and content. Art as armchair, as a cozy respite for the businessman (not, it must be emphasized, the working-class manual laborer): what metaphor could be more insulting to the self-appointed guardians of the early-twentieth-century avant-garde?

This quote from Matisse has been variably defended and dissected at great length by many others, including those who attempt to contextualize it within artist's larger project about opticality, line, and color (e.g., Hilton Kramer) as well as by feminist critics who use it as ammunition in their arguments about his misogynistic representations of women and his presumption of a male spectator (e.g., Jo Anna Isaak).[2] For Isaak, Matisse's Orientalizing odalisques and many of his other representations of women portray them as little more than the static objects, no better, and, in fact, frequently rendered

1 Henri Matisse, "Notes d'un Peintre" in *La Grande Revue* (Paris, December 25, 1908); as translated by Jack Flam in *Matisse on Art* (Berkeley: University of California Press, 1995), 42.

2 Hilton Kramer, "Reflection on Matisse," *The New Criterion* 11, no. 3 (November 1992): 4; Jo Anna Isaak, *Feminism and Contemporary Art: The Revolutionary Power of Women's Laughter* (London and New York: Routledge, 1996).

with less detail and attention, than his depictions of armchairs. By contrast, recent feminist artists, Isaak states, "have been calling into question the nature of the comfort to be had from the 'comfortable chair' of culture, revealing that for some this has been the site of acute discomfort."[3] Isaak's point is well taken, yet the vitriol that has accompanied most discussions of Matisse's passage also tells us something about the long-vexed relationship between elevated fine art such as painting and the humble functionality of furniture—any whiff that a painting might be as usable as a chair or a table demeans it, lowering it to the status of mere stuff. But what does the comparison demean more? The painting, which has become nothing more than an instrument of relaxation? The viewer, who seeks only pleasure and resists challenge? Or the maligned chair itself?

In the canny pairing of the paintings of Ginny Casey and the sculpture of Jessi Reaves, we have a different model on offer of a relationship between viewers, art, and household goods: a feminist understanding of how the objects around us, the ones that surround us in our homes, shape our everyday interactions and might enliven, or trouble, how we occupy shared space. Both knowingly look back at and re-signify key motifs and materials from the history of art. Both partake of what could be called a post-Surrealism visual vocabulary, in which the ordinary is made strange. Both grasp how the charged discourses of the domestic and the decorative have long been feminized. Both use strategies of fantasy, dislocation, and excess (including surprising textural contrasts that press together the animate and the inanimate, a dreamlike sense of scale, and a conjoining of high and low references) to push what could be familiar into the terrain of both humor and derangement. Taken together, their projects form a complex and nuanced statement about the ambivalence of domesticity, its capacities to confine as well as to nurture.

3 Isaak, *Feminism and Contemporary Art*, 55.

Chairs, for instance, do more than offer support for weary businessmen; as Isaak reminds us with her observation about "acute discomfort," they also train unruly subjects to sit in certain ways. Chairs are charged by codes of ableism—not every body fits easily into a chair, especially one with confining armrests. They can dictate how closely we are able to get to others when pulled up around a table; they can prescribe certain shapes to which our flesh must conform.

Drawing from art-historical references such as Kay Sage and Philip Guston, Casey fills her picture planes with muscular, anthropomorphized things: fragmented, disembodied hands and feet that could be sculptures or amputated body parts, eerie and visceral vessels that appear to be conspiring amongst themselves, quotidian items clustered together in disorienting configurations inhabiting oddly spatialized rooms. In one painting, a ladder climbs up the side of a giant urn, beckoning us to imagine what might be inside, while in another, a tabletop is laden with the remains of smashed vase and an outsize hammer (*Blue Vase with Ladder*, 2016; *Broken Vase*, 2015). Though these works clearly refer to the careful arrangements of meaningful items characteristic of the still life—which has often been understood to occupy the lowest rung on the hierarchy of genres within Western traditions of painting since the seventeenth century—these compositions are hardly inert. Rather, they teem with activity both implicit and explicit. Sometimes, Casey's paintings self-reflexively comment on the work of making art itself by thematizing the site of the studio. In particular, she draws from the language of ceramics as she shows wire cutters, the beginnings of a coil pot, and the molding of clay to gesture to an affinity between sculptural procedures and her own painterly carving out of volumetric spaces (*Pressing Matter*, 2015; *The Potter's Ear*, 2015).

In Casey's *Blue Table*, 2016, a scene of destruction unfolds: a saw is cutting into the surface of a lozenge-shaped table as a white upholstered chair serves as a proximate witness. Or maybe we are seeing a pause in the implicit action: perhaps someone started to cut the table, then wandered off-scene, leaving the saw in place. Though the canvas is devoid of literal people, it would be a mischaracterization to state that there is no human presence invoked here: the real-world counterparts of these images of chair, table, and saw are all tethered to the many phantom bodies that labored to create them, design them, and arrange them—and then translated deftly by Casey's own hand. As Sara Ahmed writes in her book *Queer Phenomenology*: "The table has a certain form, as we know. It is made of something (perhaps wood). The matter and form of the table are dependent upon histories of labor, which are congealed in and as the very 'thing' of the table. The table is an effect of work, and it also points to work in the very form that it takes."[4] Tables, for Casey, are special kinds of support—she uses them to suggest acts of creation and obliteration as well as to play with perspective to disorient the viewers about where, exactly, we are located. She often fully tips her tabletops up against the picture plane to allow us access to their entire surfaces, whether strewn with broken crockery or in the midst of being sawed into pieces.

Like Casey, Reaves often plunges us into the discomfiting place of the domestic; she proposes that the home and its furnishings should not be understood as straightforward respite or oasis, but rather as a site that can be undergirded by loss, disturbance, and fragility. Yet as with the work of Casey, these more somber qualities are frequently leavened by wit; for *More Personal Headboard*, 2017, Reaves has grafted a writhing fabric snake around the top edge of a wooden headboard. The brown and green intestinal forms, lashed together with green fiber, function as an incongruous addition to the top edge of the rough unfinished wood, like a flourish of thick ribbons of icing squeezed from a tube. In *Deals 3 Damage (Wicker Shelf)*, 2016, she adds

4 Sara Ahmed, *Queer Phenomenology: Orientations, Objects, Others* (Durham and London: Duke University Press, 2006), 49.

lumps of fleshy foam onto a wicker skeleton, suggesting a raw inner life. Her sculptural furniture—which retains its functionality—traffics in some signature Surrealist tropes, including an anthropomorphism both charming and chilling. Because her *Smushed Butt Table*, 2016, merges person and thing—its top is inverted as it becomes evocative of the flattened ass-cheeks of a human bottom—it flirts with the grotesque, placing what is coded as private on full view. Both *More Personal Headboard* and *Smushed Butt Table* poke fun at the bespoke culture of "personalized" furniture, in which eccentricities or less-than-desirable qualities become sedimented into our stuff.

Ahmed writes extensively about what it means to face or direct oneself towards a table, that is, to write, to eat, and to congregate around one. For Ahmed, the table is the site of communal gathering but also can be a locus of the policing of gender and sexuality, for correct comportment and obedience to the Law. In resistance to the patriarchal, heterosexual table, she conjures a feminist and queer table, one that might be activated by touch and allows subjects to reorient themselves around it in more intimate configurations. This turns in part on understanding that the table has not just a "top" but a "face," and we must be accountable to "*how we face the face, or how we are faced.*" She writes: "If the face of the table is oriented, if it acquires its significance in how it points to us, then the table disorientates when it no longer faces the right way." For Ahmed, that disorientation is critical to the formation of different socialities, as it can prompt other forms of alliance. "Queer gatherings are lines that gather—on the face, or as bodies around the table—to form new patterns and new ways of making sense."[5] Ahmed's notion of the table as a queer face resonates both with Casey's reoriented surfaces and with Reaves's sculptural work as it rethinks what a body might be.

In addition, Reaves's work literally generates non-normative gathering spaces—her plush curved ottoman hugs

5 Ahmed, 171.

a corner and offers itself as seating to be used (*Ottoman with Parked Chair & Ottoman*, 2017). Pieced together from upholsteries with distinctly different class registers, such as floral fabrics that read as "low," and incorporating other "high" furniture including a Marcel Breuer chrome and caning chair, the ottoman is a manifesto on the vitality that comes from blurring high/low distinctions. Indeed, Reaves is compelled by a feminist imperative to make visible the lower registers of furniture, including those affiliated with the "women's work" of craft and textile components, juxtaposing them with ready-made examples of high design like Breuer. In *Slipcovered Chair (Pink Gag)*, 2017, she takes the instantly recognizable Breuer B64 chair and alters it with a cheekily feminizing addition of a hot-pink slipcover. Originally manufactured in the 1920s and available for purchase for twenty-four dollars, the B64 is now known as the Cesca chair and prized by collectors. Breuer never patented the chair's design, so over the last century it has become one of the most common templates for chair design, thus simultaneously signaling pure modernist pedigree and, paradoxically, ubiquity and endless replication.[6] Reaves turns to it precisely for this contradiction, while her deployment of caning also harkens back to its importance for the history of art, notably its incorporation within Pablo Picasso's and Georges Braque's early collage work.

Reaves's *Chair 1* and *Chair 2*, both from 2016, were made by weaving together organic and fabricated materials (gnarled sticks of driftwood, foam, and plastic). The twisting cloth stands in for tendon and muscle, while the bowed wooden chair legs have a prosthetic feel. Placed side by side, the two chairs become surrogate bodies, not identical twins but kin of some sort, inviting viewers to sit and engage in their own one-on-one conversation. These chairs, which have been evidently labored over, and whose jutting edges do not look, at first glance, entirely welcoming, bring us back to that overdetermined cultural

6 Elaine Louie, "The Many Lives of a Very Common Chair," *New York Times* (February 7, 1991).

site, Matisse's relaxing armchair. Against Matisse, the pairing of Casey and Reaves thwarts assumptions about the long-vexed relationship—some would even call it a feud—between art and furniture. They investigate the sphere of the domestic, mining it for its dark comedies and its unsettling proximities. Ahmed's queer table displaces Matisse's armchair as a touchstone for Casey and Reaves alike—whether invoking the potter's worksite or crafting a corporeal nightstand—and viewers of all kinds are invited to gather around.

Exhibition Checklist

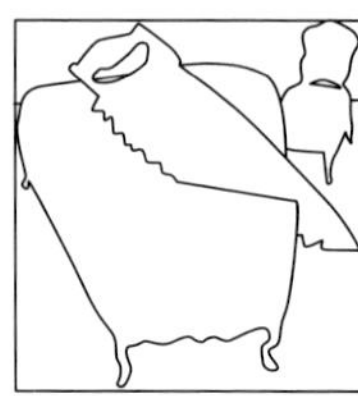

Ginny Casey, *Blue Table*, 2016
Oil on canvas, 32 × 30 in.
Collection of
Half Gallery, New York

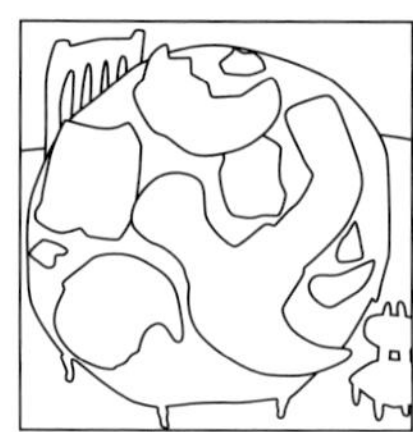

Ginny Casey, *Broken Vase*, 2015
Oil on canvas, 55 × 55 in.
Collection of Bill Powers
and Cynthia Rowley

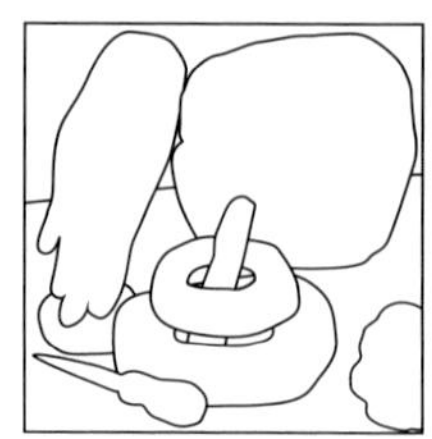

Ginny Casey,
Pressing Matter, 2015
Oil on canvas, 55 × 55 in.
Private Collection

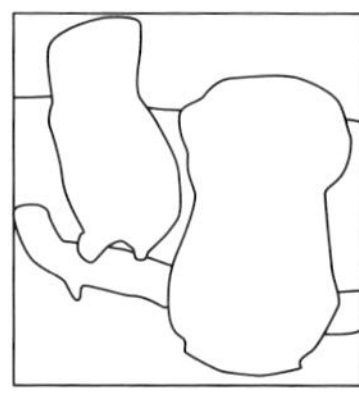

Ginny Casey,
Purple Conversation, 2016
Oil on canvas, 32 × 30 in.
Private Collection

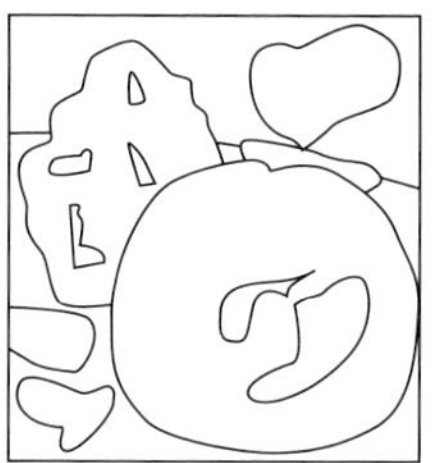

Ginny Casey,
Sculpture Studio, 2016
Oil on canvas, 56 × 53 in.
Courtesy the artist and
Half Gallery, New York

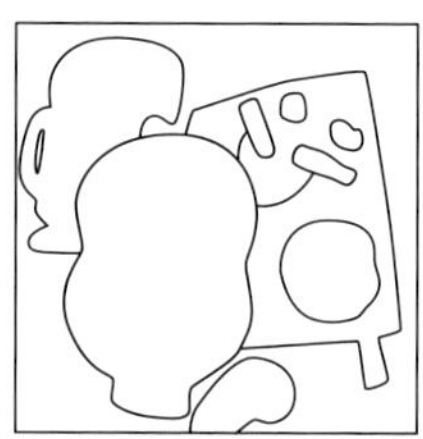

Ginny Casey,
The Potter's Ear, 2015
Oil on canvas, 55 × 55 in.
Private Collection, New York

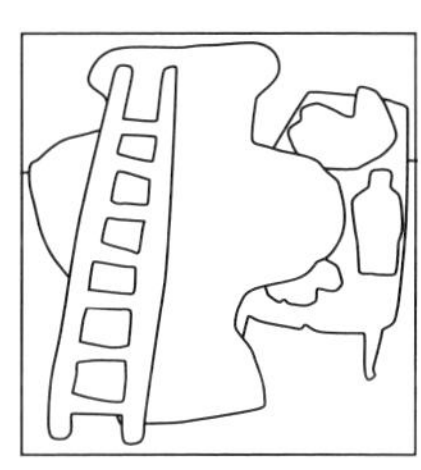

Ginny Casey,
Blue Vase with Ladder, 2016
Oil on canvas, 56 × 53 in.
Private Collection

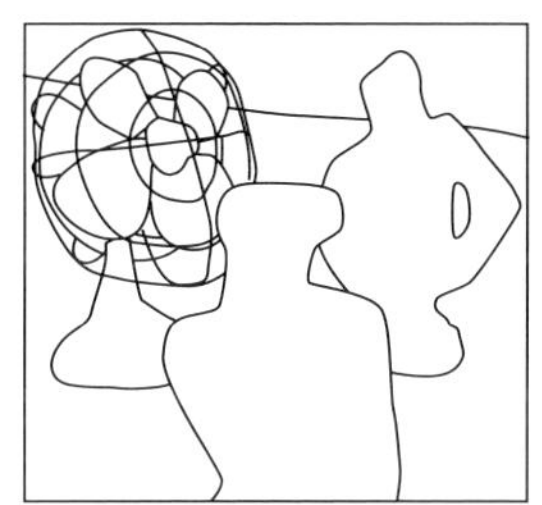

Ginny Casey,
Fan with Jugs, 2017
Oil on canvas, 56 × 60 in.
Courtesy the artist and
Half Gallery, New York

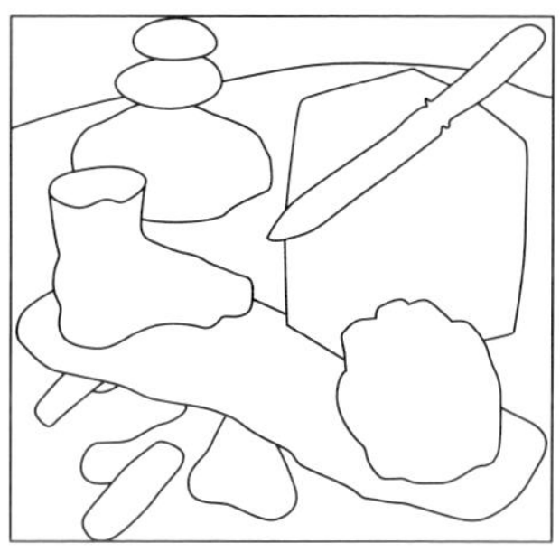

Ginny Casey,
Balancing Act, 2017
Oil on canvas, 70 × 75 in.
Courtesy the artist
and Half Gallery, New York

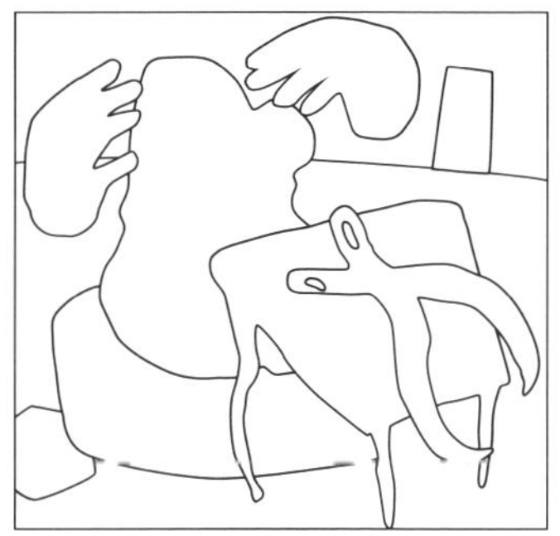

Ginny Casey,
Moody Blue Studio, 2017
Oil on canvas, 70 × 75 in.
Courtesy the artist
and Half Gallery, New York

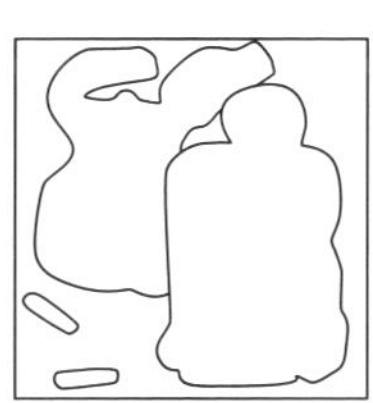

Ginny Casey,
Chatty Forms, 2016
Oil on canvas, 30 × 30 in.
Private Collection

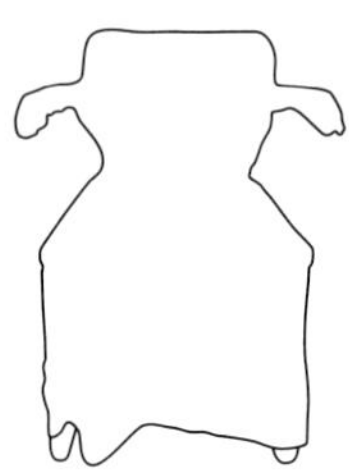

Jessi Reaves, *Slipcovered Chair (Pink Gag)*, 2017
Found chair, fabric, zipper, and thread, 33 × 22 × 24 in.
Courtesy the artist and Bridget Donahue, New York

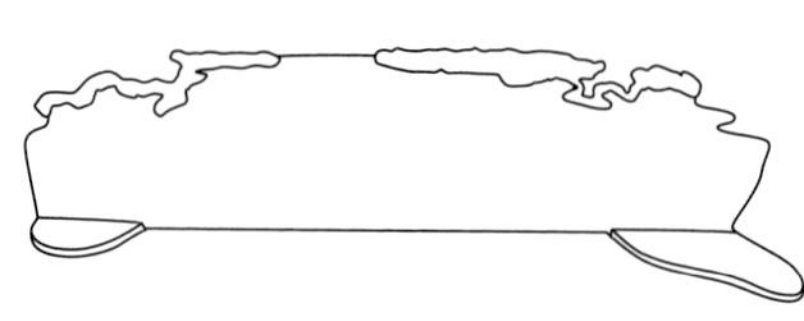

Jessi Reaves,
More Personal Headboard, 2017
Plywood, sawdust, wood glue, foam, silk, nylon cord, ink, and wood putty, 24 × 98 × 13.5 in.
Courtesy the artist and Bridget Donahue, New York

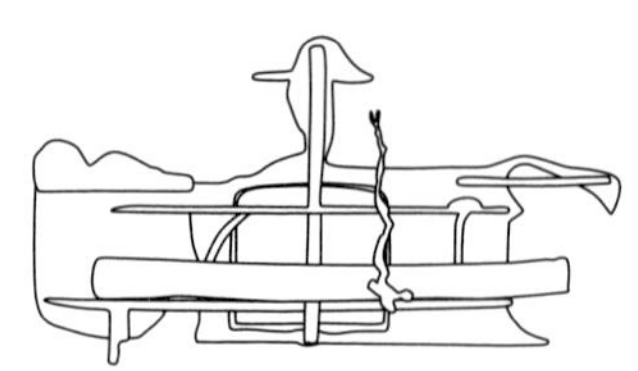

Jessi Reaves,
Shelf for a Log, 2016
Plywood, sawdust, cane chair seat, and ink, 34 × 68 × 13 in.
Private Collection

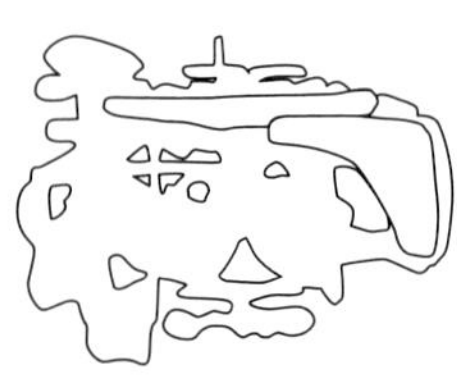

Jessi Reaves,
Shelf with Pockets & Braid, 2017
Plywood, driftwood, bondfire wood, sawdust, wood glue, chair caning, metal, leather, velvet, silk, and ink, 39 × 50 × 12 in.
Courtesy the artist and Bridget Donahue, New York

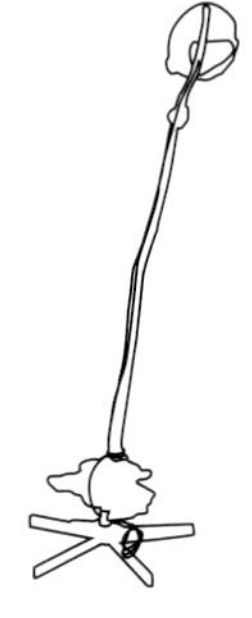

Jessi Reaves,
Worthless Lump (Lamp), 2017
Chair base, bun foot, plywood, sawdust, wood glue, driftwood, lamp wiring, and lamp shade (steel silk), 90 × 40 × 22 in.
Courtesy the artist and Bridget Donahue, New York

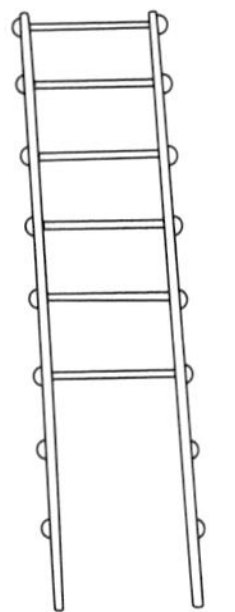

Jessi Reaves, *sexy hazard ladder*, 2015
Chair base, bun foot, plywood, sawdust, wood glue, driftwood, lamp wiring, and lamp shade (steel silk), 96 × 24 × 4 in.
Courtesy the artist and Bridget Donahue, New York

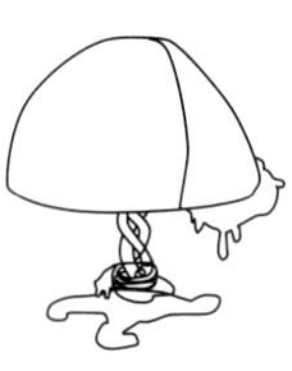

Jessi Reaves,
Split Mess (Barley Twist Lamps), 2017
Wood, metal, fabric, sawdust, wood-glue, upholstery trim, velour beads, thread, lamp wiring, and LED bulbs, 21 × 16 × 16 in.
Courtesy the artist and Bridget Donahue, New York

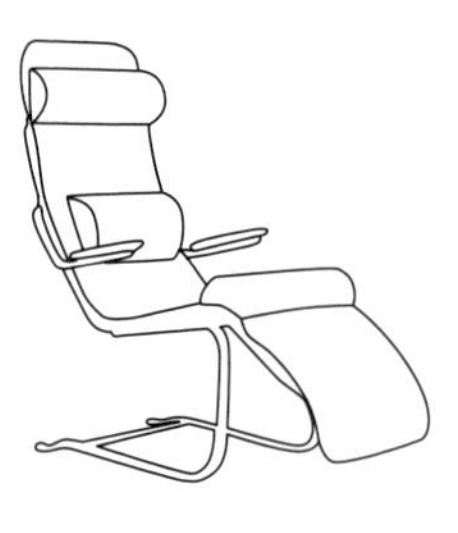

Jessi Reaves,
Kragel's Nap Chair, 2015
Steel, rattan, enamel, polyurethane foam, cotton, ink, plastic glass, and hardware, 47 × 24½ × 48 in.
Collection of Susan Cianciolo

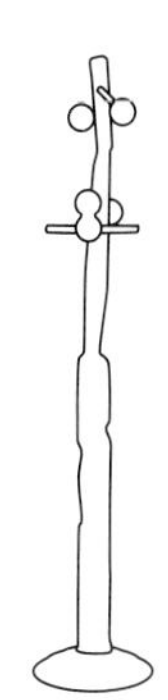

Jessi Reaves,
Dog's Toy Coat Rack, 2015
Canadian oak, steel, and varnish,
72 × 14¼ × 14¼ in.
Private Collection, New York

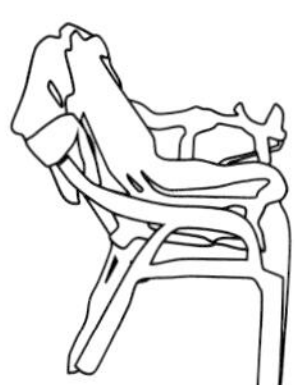

Jessi Reaves, *Chair 1* and
Chair 2, 2016
Plastic, driftwood, sawdust,
wood glue, fabric, cotton,
batting, and polyurethane foam,
38 × 25 × 29 in.; 38 × 27 × 22 in.
Courtesy the artist and
Bridget Donahue, New York

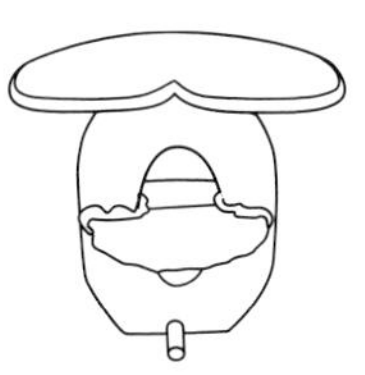

Jessi Reaves, *Smushed Butt
Table*, 2016
Plywood, pine, rubber,
polyurethane foam, plastic,
and ink, 30 × 30 × 28 in.
Private Collection

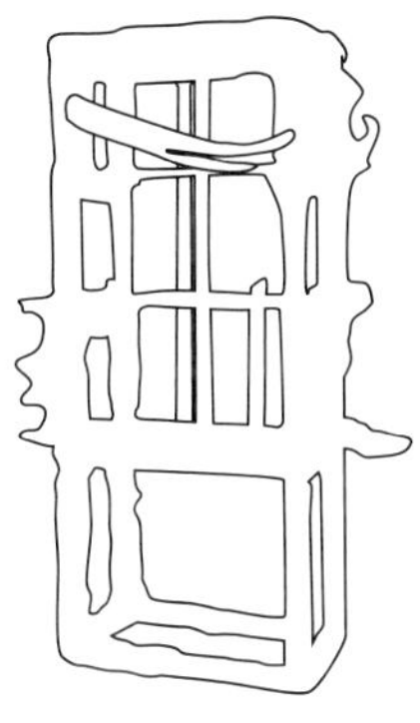

Jessi Reaves, *Deals 3 Damage
(Wicker Shelf)*, 2016
Wood, wicker, plywood, studio
dust, wood glue,
polyurethane foam, ink,
and hardware, 84 × 48 × 24 in.
Collection of Scott J. Lorinsky

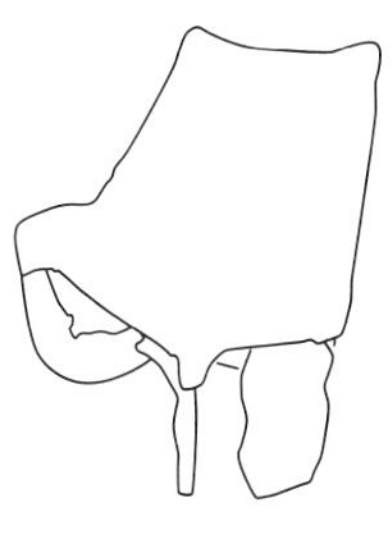

Jessi Reaves, *Mutant
Butterfly Chair*, 2017
Plywood, leather, plastic,
hardware, wood, sawdust,
and wood glue, 34 × 40 × 41 in.
Courtesy the artist and
Bridget Donahue, New York

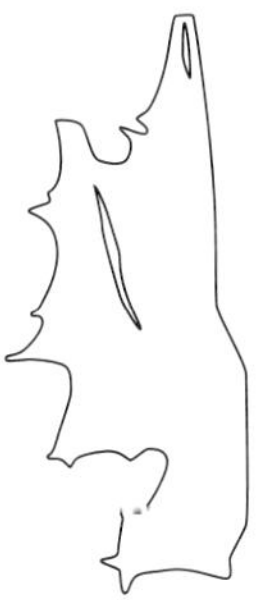

Jessi Reaves, *Night Cabinet
(Little Miss Attitude)*, 2016
Plywood, wood, steel, silk,
and zippers, 72 × 32 × 26 in.
Courtesy the artist and
Bridget Donahue, New York

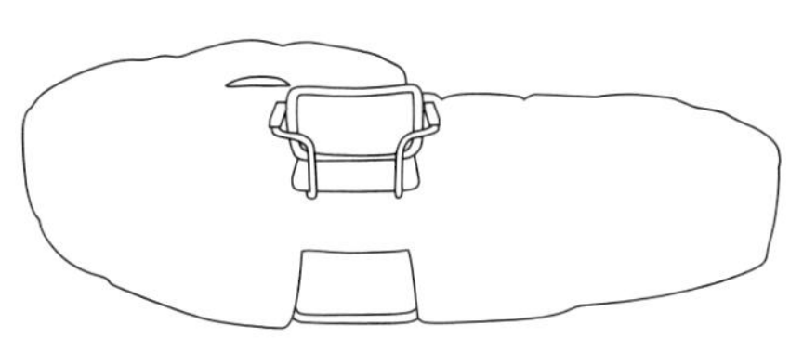

Jessi Reaves, *Ottoman with
Parked Chair & Ottoman*, 2017
Plywood, foam, fleece, fabric, hardware,
and found furniture, 111 × 130 × 19 in.
Courtesy the artist and
Bridget Donahue, New York

18: Jessi Reaves, *Anyone Knows How It Happened (Headboard for One)*, 2016, plywood, foam, plastiwood, and hardware, 49 × 94 × 19 inches. Courtesy the artist and Bridget Donahue; **21:** Jessi Reaves, *Cesca Leaves the Stacks (Modified Chair)*, 2016, polyurethane foam, tubular steel frame chrome plated finish, hardwood beech with cane inserts, rayon, nylon, plastic, ink, and hardware, 48 × 18$\frac{1}{4}$ × 28 inches. Courtesy the artist and Bridget Donahue, New York; **22:** Marcel Breuer, Cesca Armchair (model B64), 1928, bent chromed tubular steel, wood, and cane, 30$\frac{7}{8}$ × 22$\frac{7}{8}$ × 23$\frac{1}{4}$ inches. Manufactured by Gebrüder Thonet, Vienna. Collection of The Museum of Modern Art, New York; Gift of Manfred Ludewig. Photo: © The Museum of Modern Art / Licensed by SCALA / Art Resource, New York; Jessi Reaves, *if you want to know what will bring you back to life, it's nothing*, 2014, wood, foam, nylon, beads, piping, and pearls, 39 × 25 × 27 inches. Courtesy the artist and Bridget Donahue, New York. Photo: Marc Brems Tatti; **26:** Willi Baumeister, *Wie Wohnen? Die Wohnung Werkbund Ausstellung*, 1927, offset lithograph, 44$\frac{3}{4}$ × 32$\frac{3}{8}$ inches. Collection of The Museum of Modern Art, New York; Gift of Philip Johnson. © Artist Rights Society (ARS), New York / VG Bild-Kunst, Bonn, 2017. Photo: The Museum of Modern Art / Licensed by SCALA / Art Resource, New York; **30:** Charlotte Perriand, *Charlotte Perriand resting on the chaise lounge*, 1928, photograph. Designed by Le Corbusier, Charlotte Perriand, and Pierre Jeanneret. DR – Archives Charlotte Perriand. © Artist Rights Society (ARS), New York / ADAGP, Paris, 2017. Photo: Banque d'Images, ADAGP / Art Resource, New York; Pierre Jeanneret and Le Corbusier, Pavillon de l'Esprit Nouveau, 1925, *Exposition Internationale des Arts Décoratifs et Industriels Modernes* – Musée des Arts décoratifs (fonds éditions Albert Lévy). © F.L.C. / ADAGP, Paris / Artist Rights Society (ARS), New York, 2017. Photo: © Paris, Les Arts Décoratifs / Thibaud, 1925; **33:** Ginny Casey, *Keeping Time*, 2017, oil on canvas, 70 × 65 inches. Courtesy the artist and Half Gallery, New York; Ginny Casey, *Droopy Vase*, 2015, oil on canvas, 55 × 55 inches. Private Collection. Courtesy the artist and Half Gallery, New York; **34:** Brassaï, *Le Corbusier at his work table, rue Jacob*, 1931, photograph. Private Collection. © Estate Brassaï—RMN-Grand Palais © F.L.C. / ADAGP / Art Resource, NY. Photo: © RMN-Grand Palais / Michèle Bellot; **37:** Méret Oppenheim, *Table with Bird's Legs*, 1938–39. Made by Simon International, possibly in Italy, 1972–84. Collection of Victoria and Albert Museum, London. © Artist Rights Society (ARS), New York / ProLitteris, Zurich, 2017. Photo: © Victoria and Albert Museum, London; **38:** Ginny Casey, *Hat and Scarf*, 2015, oil on canvas, 24 × 20 inches. Courtesy the artist and Half Gallery, New York; **41:** Jessi Reaves, *Quick-To-Sew Jester's Hat (Noguchi Knockoff #1)*, 2016, cedar chips, sawdust, wood, glass, and pewter paint, 15 × 40 inches. Courtesy the artist and Bridget Donahue, New York; **42:** Jessi Reaves, *Foam Couch with Straps*, 2016, upholstery foam, fiberglass, wood, and webbing, 29 × 77 × 35 inches. Courtesy the artist and Bridget Donahue, New York; **45:** Salvador Dalí, *Mae West's Face which May be Used as a Surrealist Apartment*, 1934–35, gouache with graphite, on commercially printed magazine page, 11 × 7 inches. Collection of The Art Institute of Chicago; Gift of Mrs. Charles B. Goodspeed. © Salvador Dalí, Fundació Gala-Salvador Dalí, Artist Rights Society (ARS), New York, 2017. Photo: The Art Institute of Chicago / Art Resource, New York; Salvador Dalí and Oscar Tusquets Blanca, *Mae West Room*, c. 1974, installation. © Salvador Dalí, Fundació Gala-Salvador Dalí /Artist Rights Society (ARS), New York, 2017; **49:** Man Ray, *Indestructible Object (or Object to Be Destroyed)*, 1964 (replica of 1923 original), metronome with cutout photograph of eye on pendulum, 8$\frac{7}{8}$ × 4$\frac{3}{8}$ × 4$\frac{5}{8}$ inches. Collection of The Museum of Modern Art, New York; James Thrall Soby Fund. © Man Ray Trust / Artist Rights Society (ARS), New York / ADAGP, Paris, 2017. Photo: © The Museum of Modern Art / Licensed by SCALA / Art Resource, New York; **51:** Jessi Reaves, *Idol of the Hares*, 2014, oak, polyurethane foam, silk, cotton, aluminum, and ink, 38 × 28 × 48 inches. Courtesy the artist and Bridget Donahue, New York. Photo: Marc Brems Tatti; **57:** *International Exhibition of Modern Art*, 1926–27, installation view, Brooklyn Museum. Yale Collection of American Literature, Beinecke Rare Book and Manuscript Library, Yale University, New Haven, CT; **58:** Study designed by Pierre Chareau for an exhibition on French decorative arts at Lord and Taylor, New York, 1928. Dorothy Shaver Papers, Archives Center, National Museum of American History, Smithsonian Institution, Washington, D.C.; *Play Things*, 2016, installation view, Half Gallery, New York. Courtesy Half Gallery, New York. Photo: Martin Parsekian; **61:** *Improbable Furniture*, 1977, installation view, Institute of Contemporary Art, University of Pennsylvania.

Published on the occasion of
Ginny Casey & Jessi Reaves
April 28–August 6, 2017

Institute of Contemporary Art
University of Pennsylvania
118 S. 36th Street
Philadelphia, PA 19104-3289
www.icaphila.org

Copy Editor: Abraham Adams
Photography: Constance Mensh
Design: Practise (James Goggin with William Sumrall)
Checklist Illustrations: Other Means
Edition of 500
ISBN: 978-0-88454-141-7
Library of Congress Cataloging-in-Publication Data can be obtained at the Library of Congress

Funding for *Ginny Casey & Jessi Reaves* and for ICA's Whitney-Lauder Curatorial Fellow Program has been provided by the Leonard & Judy Lauder Fund of The Lauder Foundation.

ICA is always free. For all. Free admission is courtesy of Amanda and Glenn Fuhrman.

ICA acknowledges the generous sponsorship of Barbara B. & Theodore R. Aronson for exhibition catalogues. Programming at ICA has been made possible in part by the Emily and Jerry Spiegel fund to support contemporary culture and visual arts and the Lise Spiegel-Wilks and Jeffrey Wilks family foundation, and by Hilarie L. & Mitchell Morgan. Marketing is supported by Pamela Toub Berkman & David J. Berkman and by Lisa A. & Steven A. Tananbaum. Additional funding has been provided by the Horace W. Goldsmith Foundation, the Dietrich Foundation and the Daniel W. Dietrich II Trust, Inc., the overseers board for the Institute of Contemporary Art, friends and members of ICA, and the University of Pennsylvania council on the arts, a state agency funded by the commonwealth of Pennsylvania and the National Endowment for the Arts, a federal agency. ICA acknowledges Le Méridien Philadelphia as our official Unlock Art™ partner hotel.

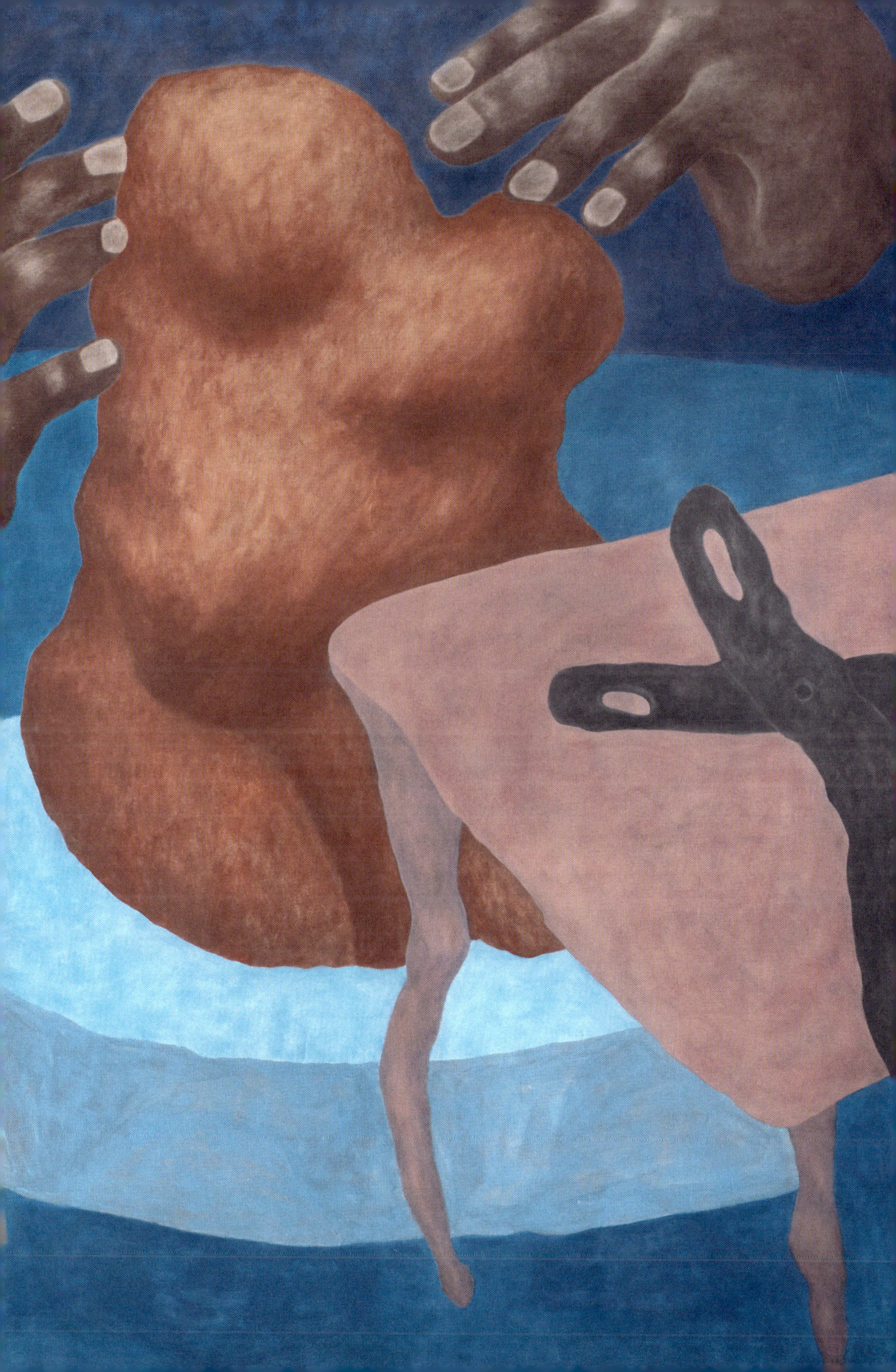

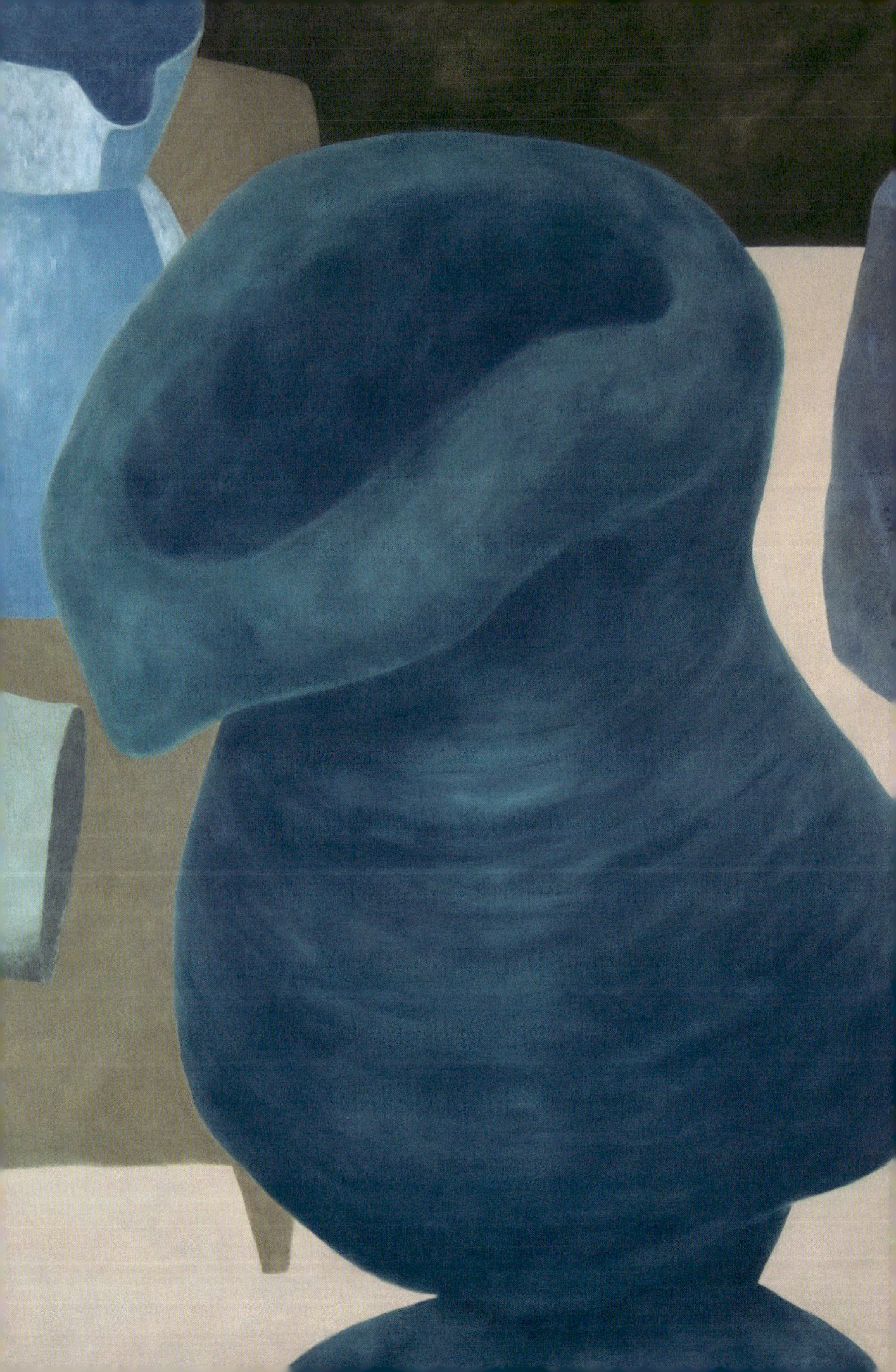

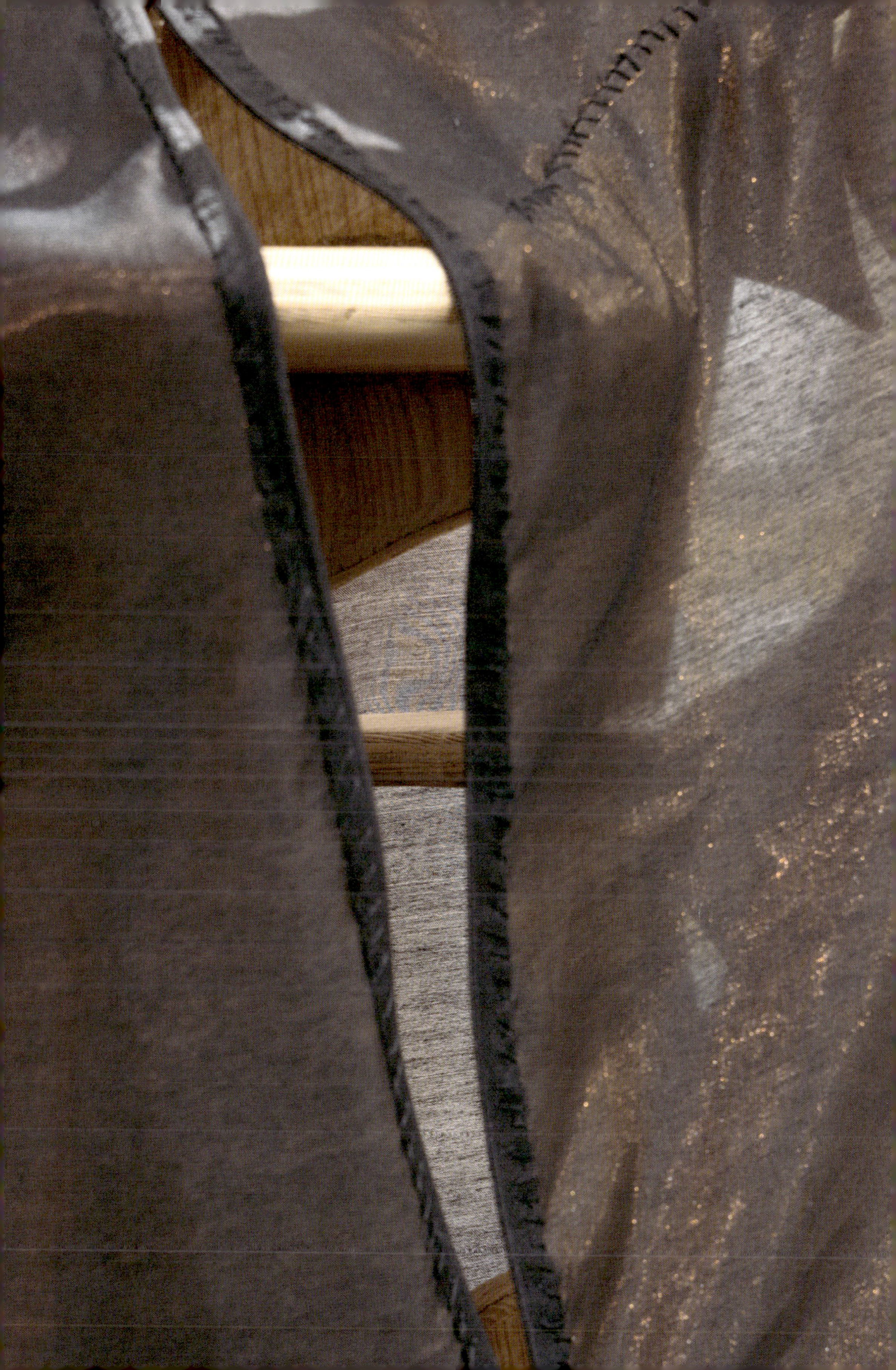

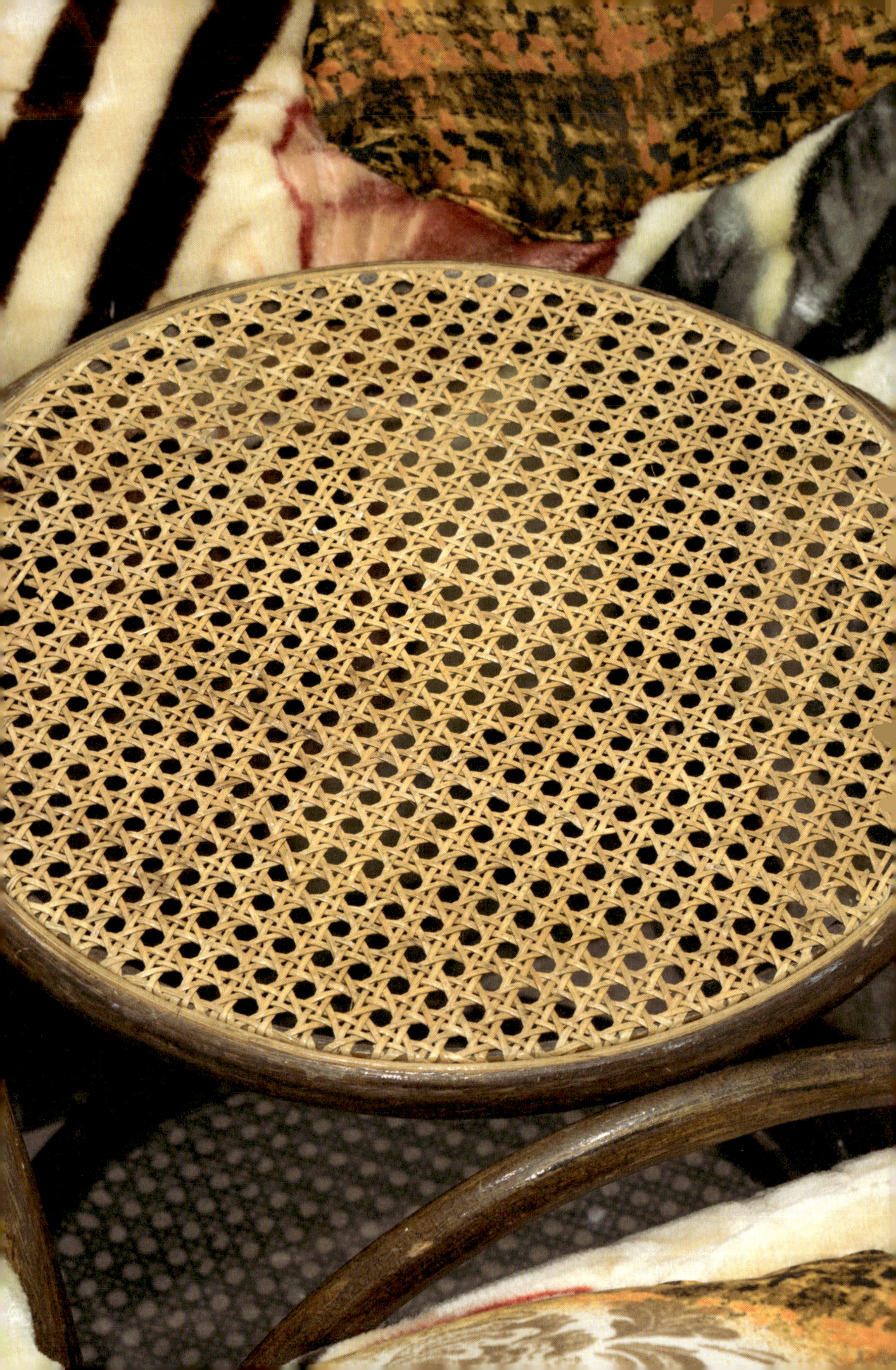

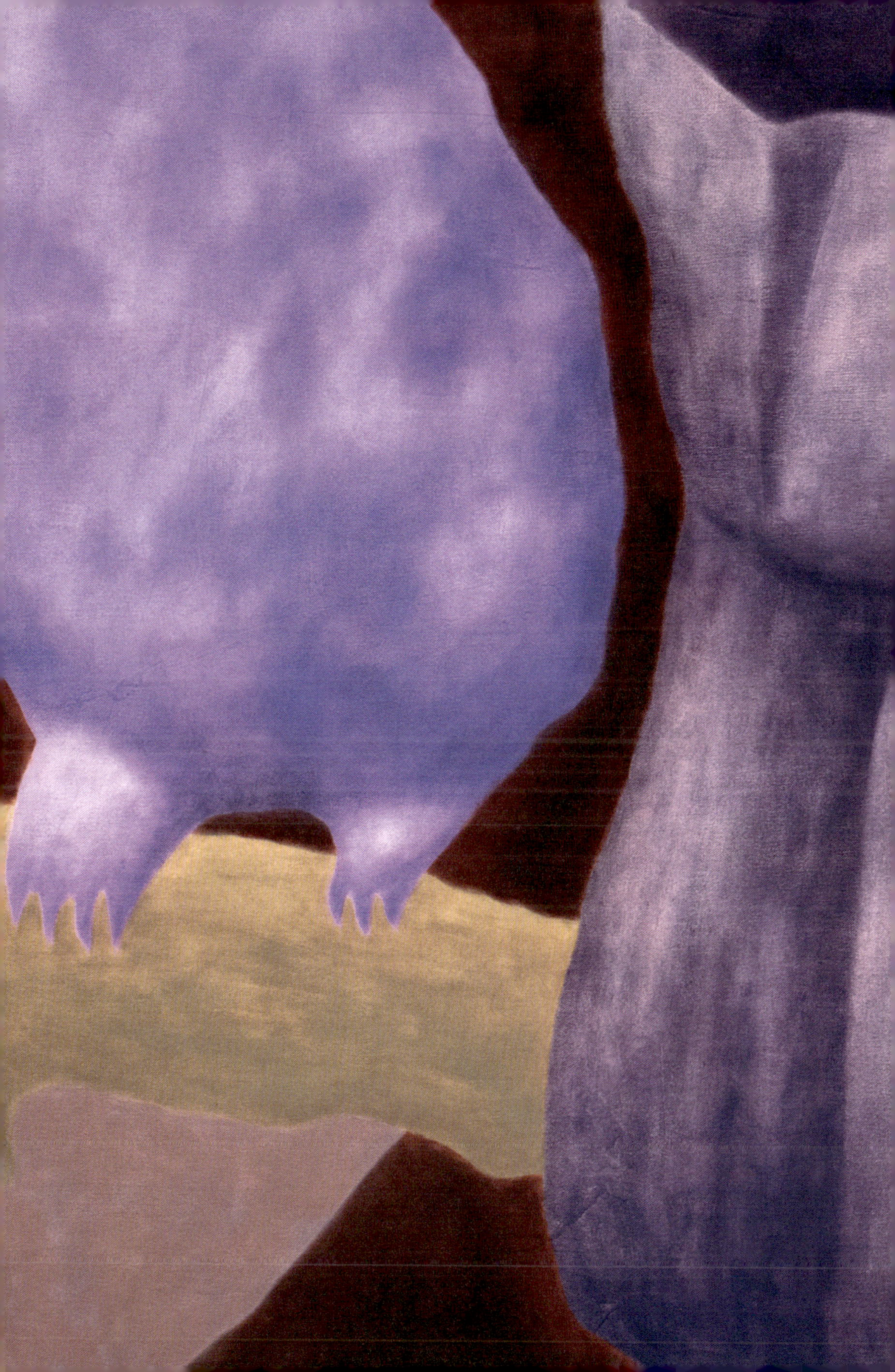

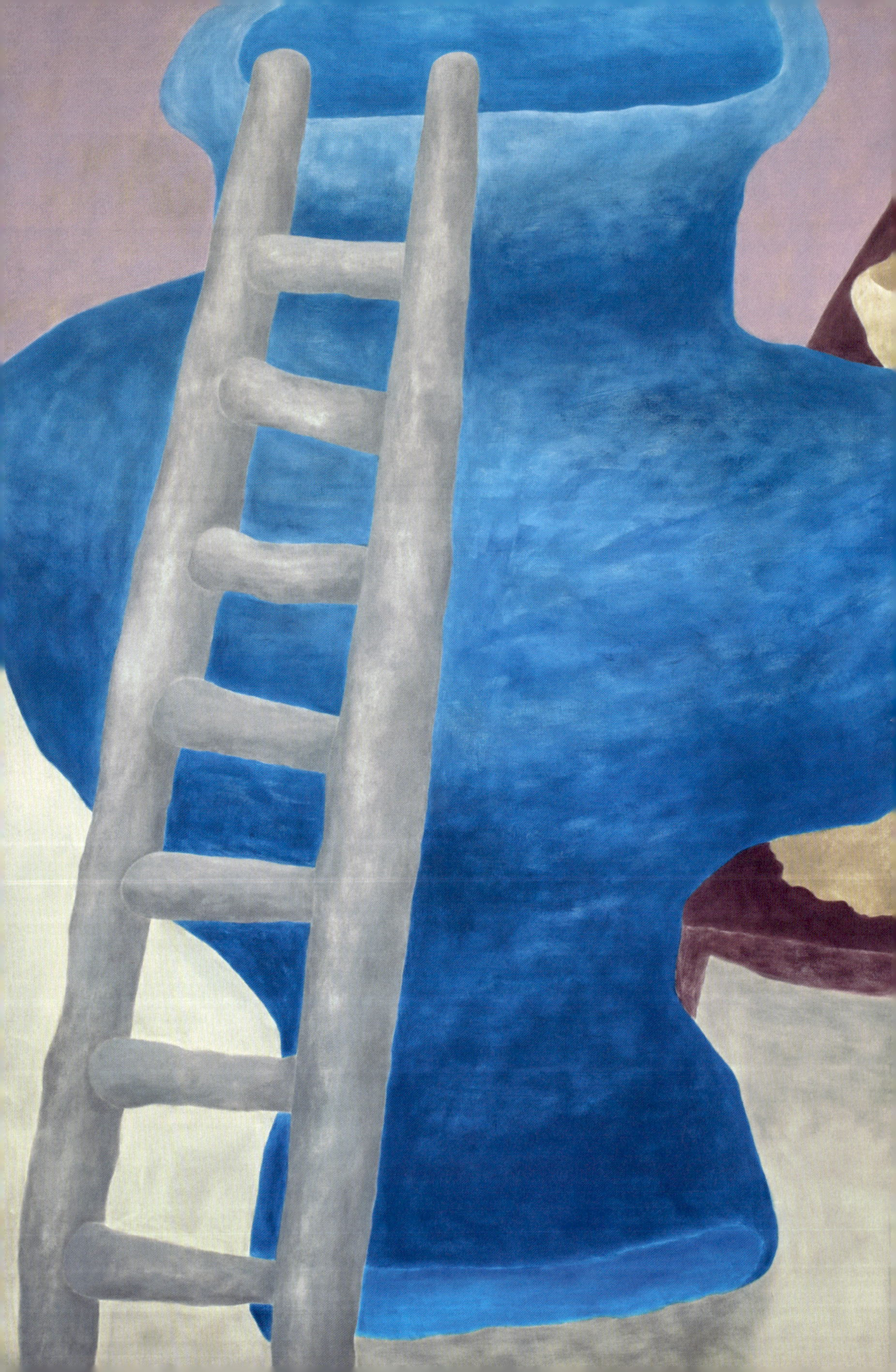